*f*P

HIGH-CONFLICT, VIOLENT, AND SEPARATING FAMILIES

A Group Treatment Manual for School-Age Children

Vivienne Roseby, Ph.D., and Janet R. Johnston, Ph.D.

THE FREE PRESS

NEW YORK   LONDON   TORONTO   SYDNEY   SINGAPORE

THE FREE PRESS
A Division of Simon & Schuster Inc.
1230 Avenue of the Americas
New York, NY 10020

THE FREE PRESS and colophon are trademarks of Simon & Schuster Inc.

Designed by gumption design

Manufactured in the United States of America

10 9 8 7 6 5 4 3 2 1

Library of Congress Cataloging-in-Publication Data

Roseby, Vivienne. 1951–
    High-conflict, violent, and separating families : a group treatment
manual for school-age children / Vivienne Roseby and Janet R.
Johnston.
        p. cm.
    A revision of author's thesis (Ph. D.)—University of Wisconsin.
    Includes index.
    ISBN 0-684-82769-7(alk. paper)
    1. Problem families.   2. Group psychotherapy for children.
3. Schemas (Psychology) in children.   I. Johnston, Janet R.
II. Title.
RJ507.F33R67   1997
618.92'85822—DC21   97-10284
                                                    CIP

This manual is dedicated to my husband, Herb Berkoff, who supported me at every step along the way.

—Vivienne Roseby

ACKNOWLEDGMENTS

The original version of this manual was funded by a state assigned fellowship for dissertation research to Vivienne Roseby, Ph.D. from the University of Wisconsin Graduate School of Education. This revised version was supported, in part, with funds from the Marin Community Foundation, the Zellerbach Family Fund, and the Van Loben Sels Foundation. We would like to acknowledge the invaluable contributions of Dr. Robin Deutsch to the original version of this manual. We are also indebted to Dr. Judith Wallerstein and the staff of the Judith Wallerstein Center for the Family in Transition for their constant interest and support in this work. We would also like to thank Barbara Lehman for her incisive editorial assistance and her humor. Finally, we are deeply grateful to all of the children and families who participated in our groups, and who allowed us to learn as we went along.

CONTENTS

TABLES AND FIGURES

INTRODUCTION

This manual presents a unique, step-by-step model for treating school-age children in divorcing, highly conflicted, or violent families. This model was developed at one of the country's foremost centers for family research, the Judith Wallerstein Center for the Family in Transition, and is based on the authors' more than twenty combined years of experience with these children and their families. The model represents a practical application of theory to the treatment of particular developmental difficulties that arise in this population.

ABOUT THIS TREATMENT APPROACH

What developmental difficulties are addressed in this approach?

Children who live in conflicted or violent divorcing families often experience their primary relationships as frighteningly unpredictable and double binding. These children appear to manage the resulting anxiety by narrowing their feelings and ideas about themselves, other people, and relationships into very simple and rigid patterns. With time these patterns seem to consolidate into internal *scripts*. The scripts are built around each child's unique experiences, and contain unconscious rules and expectations that shape and control perceptions, feelings, thoughts, and behavior. This kind of inner rigidity serves to maximize the child's sense of safety and predictability. Typically children cannot express their internal scripts in words, but will play them out in projective stories, sand-tray work, and role plays. It is in these activities that we can begin to know how each child has come to understand the world of relationships and what are his or her personal rules for survival in that world.

Perhaps not surprisingly, these children tend to avoid closeness with other people because closeness might challenge their fixed ideas and bring up uncomfortable feelings. Because of this tendency to avoid closeness, these children do not learn to trust relationships. They rely instead on their script and the limited ideas and feelings that the script generates. This way they feel safe, but they fail to mature into a more realistic understanding of themselves and other people. Often their ideas about moral conduct in relationships are distorted by their internal script, placing them at increased risk for becoming violent or victimized in their adult relationships as well. Compounding the problem is the fact that these children are often so mistrustful that they are extremely difficult to engage in individual counseling or psychotherapy.

The overall goal of this manual is to present a unique treatment alternative to address these developmental difficulties in a theoretically coherent and practical way. Strategies within group sessions can also be adapted for use in individual work, most particularly with children who need a degree of structure in the early or more difficult portions of treatment. (See Appendix A for specific suggestions for adapting group strategies for individual work. See the companion volume by Janet R. Johnston and Vivienne Roseby, *In the Name of the Child: A Developmental Approach to Understanding and Helping Children of Conflicted and Violent Divorce*, Free Press. New York, 1997, for a more complete discussion of developmental difficulties in children who live with conflict and violence.)

What are the goals of this approach?

The therapeutic activities are designed to help the children to surface and revise their internal scripts and the rules and expectations that support them. Each session provides clinical direction for the leader to help each child to take notice of his or her script as it emerges in role plays, family sculpting, and related activities. As the children become more conscious of the rule-bound point of view that binds them, they are helped to consider alternative perspectives. It is this shift that can help the children begin to mature into a more realistic and flexible kind of interpersonal understanding. (For a more complete discussion of the normal development of interpersonal understanding, see Robert Selman, *The Growth of Interpersonal Understanding*, Academic Press, New York, 1980.) This core work is supported by activities in five content areas: creating common ground and safety; exploring the language and complexity of feelings; defining and understanding the self; dramatizing and revising family roles, relationships, and rules of moral conduct; and defining and revising family roles, relationships, and rules of moral conduct. The sequence of activities within this group model is summarized in Table 1 on page 15.

In each area, the structure of the activity remains constant but the content that the group works with in drawing, discussion, or dramatization is always generated by the participants. This balance of content and structure represents a middle ground between a cookbook approach, which can limit the leader's ability to respond to the unique needs and histories of each group, and an unstructured concept approach, which would not tie theory to practice in any useful way.

Why is a group model a good idea?

In the authors' experience, children who have lived with conflict show a marked preference for group over individual treatment. In group, they can reduce some of the shame about their family situation and find out that they are "not the only one." The group also provides a developmentally appropriate opportunity for school-age children to learn from and about their peers in activities rather than in conversation. As well, parents seem more willing to accept the suggestion that their child participate in group rather than a suggestion for individual work.

Is there a group model for the parents?

Children gain maximum benefit from participating in this group approach when their parents are actively working to manage or reduce their conflict and to understand and protect their children more effectively. This work is best conducted by the clinician who is leading the children's group; it is the leader's direct experience of the child in the group that underscores his or her credibility to the parents and heightens their awareness and motivation. Work with parents can be conducted individually (in conjoint or separate sessions) or in psychoeducational groups, which may be scheduled to coincide with the children's meetings and can be a cost-effective and efficient approach to the kind of collateral work with parents that best supports the children. The structure and content of psychoeducational groups for parents are described in Appendix B of this manual.

ABOUT THE PARTICIPANTS

Who can benefit from this approach?

The structure of each activity (how issues will be communicated, dramatized, drawn, or incorporated into games) is defined by step-by-step instructions for each session. However, the actual content of the issues is always generated by the children. In this way, each group can and should be a unique experience that represents the special concerns of its participants. Consequently, the manual is not limited to children who live with chronic conflict or violence. It has also been used successfully with children in the general divorcing population, where conflict tends to be time limited. We do recommend, however, that children who live in families where there is chronic conflict or violence meet in groups with other children who have had similar experiences.

What is the age range for these groups?

The groups are appropriate for children from about 7 to 13 or 14 years of age. We recommend separate groups for younger (7–9) and older (10–14) children. Some group activities are specifically labeled as suitable for younger children only, and others are labeled as suitable for the older groups.

Do older children have longer sessions than younger children?

Yes. Older children (ages 10–14) meet for 90-minute sessions, but younger children (ages 7–9) generally meet for one hour. Separate groups for these age ranges allow the leaders to tailor each group's tempo, activity, and discussion to their particular developmental capacities.

How many children should be in each group?

The groups should range in size from no less than five to no more than eight participants. Optimally they should include a balance of boys to girls. When this gender balance is not possible, the leader has to consider what mix of gender and personalities might maximize the children's sense of safety.

Should I include siblings in the same group?

When siblings fall into the same age range, the decision to include them in one group rests with the leader and his or her intake information (see below) about the family. In some cases, siblings bring comfort and support to each other in the course of the group experience. In other cases, children may have taken sides against each other in the family conflict, or one child may be overshadowed by the other. In these situations, it is preferable for each child to have a separate group experience.

What kind of intake and screening information do I need?

The group leader will need to know as much about the child's family history as possible before including the child in the group. It will be important to know, for example, how long the parents have been in conflict, and as much specific information as possible about what kind of conflict or violence the child may have witnessed or heard and at what age. This information may come from interviews with parents (conducted by phone or in person) or written questionnaires. The more details the leader has, the more he or she will be able to prompt and support each child in the group.

It will also be important for the leader to know how the child has coped with group situations in the past. This can be evaluated by means of interviews with teachers and parents. Behavior checklists can be used as well. Children who have a history of acting out (which can be difficult to manage in group settings) may not be appropriate for group treatment unless sufficient staffing support can be made available.

ABOUT THE LEADER

What qualifications should the leader have, and how many leaders should there be?

This group approach requires at least one leader who is a trained mental health professional with experience in working with children. The decision to use one or two group leaders depends on the availability of resources, the training and experience of the leaders, and the specific needs of the children in the group. One leader with a good deal of experience may be successful, particularly with more mature groups. In general, however, coleadership is recommended. Two leaders can manage acting-out behavior more effectively. Discussions between the coleaders can also provide the children with a model of conflict resolution that they may not have observed before. While at least one of the coleaders should be an experienced clinician, the other may be in training or a paraprofessional.

THE ACTIVITIES AND THE OVERALL TREATMENT PLAN

How should I prepare to lead a group?

We recommend a thorough reading of the entire manual before proceeding. This includes the introduction, each of the ten sessions, and the troubleshooting and groups for parents appendixes. A careful review will provide a working framework for using the manual responsibly and effectively. We draw particular attention to the following section, *What activity is in each session, and what is the therapeutic goal?* Here we provide an overview of the sequence of activities, the therapeutic goals that they address, and the sessions in which they appear. This overview can help the leader to tailor the pacing of activities as well as to decide which can be omitted owing to lack of time or relevance.

What activity is in each session, and what is the therapeutic goal?

The manual presents, in detail, a ten-session treatment agenda. Each session includes clearly stated goals and step-by-step procedures for activities that address the appropriate therapeutic goals for that session. The main activities within each content area, the session where the activity is scheduled, and its place within the sequence of the session (identified by a letter) are listed in Table 1. Note that some activities (those that focus on organization, housekeeping, or closure) are omitted from the table.

The sessions address five therapeutic goals:

1. Creating Common Ground and Safety

The group should be a safe place where the children can learn from and about their peers. This is especially important for youngsters who tend to control and avoid rather than form real relationships.

Rules (Session I, B). Children create a brief list of rules for safe conduct within the group. It is posted in the group room during every session.

House My Family Lives In (Session I, C). Children are asked to draw the houses that the different members of their family live in. In this activity they can find common ground as well as support for the many different forms of family.

Blind Walk (Session II, B). Each blind walker (a group member who is selected or who volunteers) is blindfolded and led through an obstacle course that the other group members create especially for him or her. The activity builds unity and trust among the children as they help each other to find their own way in the face of unknown dangers.

Relaxation (Sessions IV, A–VIII, A). The leader guides the children through a progressive relaxation exercise. This helps the children to become aware of their feeling states and provides a way to ease their physical tensions.

Group Art Project (Session IX, A). Children work together without words to build a statue using a variety of common objects, such as macaroni, straws, or fabric scraps. The leader emphasizes the value of peer support and cooperation.

2. Exploring the Language and Complexity of Feelings

Many children in conflicted families have little experience in using language to express their emotions. In part this is because feelings often seem frightening and uncontrollable: Acknowledging feelings out loud can make them seem terrifyingly personal and real. The children are thus in a significant bind because they need words in order to share their experiences with other people. Using words to express feelings also provides an alternative to acting out feelings. However, this is a means of expression that many of the children have neither witnessed nor practiced. It is important to create an environment in which the verbal expression of feelings is not only permitted and encouraged, but especially valued.

List of Feelings (Session I, D). The children brainstorm a list of feelings in response to a challenge from the leader to make the longest list that any group has ever made. The chart is posted in the group room for reference in every session.

Feelings/Color (Session I, E). The children underline each basic feeling on the feelings chart using a primary color. They then combine primary colors for more complex emotions. This allows the children to use colors as well as feeling words to communicate about feelings. The activity also introduces the group to the idea of blended feelings—a crucial idea for children whose thoughts, feelings, and ideas about people and relationships tend to be oversimplified.

Level of Feelings (Session II, C). The children complete a chart with six empty thermometers that can be filled in with color to show levels of feelings. The activity introduces the idea that feelings have different levels of intensity.

Charade of Feelings (Session II, D). Each child charades a feeling from their level-of-feelings chart. The group's task is to guess the feeling as well as the level of that feeling. The leader uses questions and discussion to help the children to understand that feelings and actions are different, and that feelings cannot be controlled or judged but actions can. It is in the domain of action that children can begin to consider the question of what is right and wrong behavior in a relationship.

Inside Me/Outside Me (Session VII, C). Children use two sheets of paper, stapled together, with an identical outline of a human figure on each sheet. The children color in the top figure with colors of the feelings they show and the bottom figure with the feelings they keep inside. The activity helps children to understand that they do not have to control their feelings and ideas quite so much if they can control how they express them to other people.

Masks (Session VII, D). Children create masks to represent the self that they show to the world. In role plays, the children put the masks on when they need them for safety and remove them when they feel safe to share their true feelings.

3. Defining and Understanding the Self

Children in high-conflict families tend to find safety in responding to the needs and expectations of other people. They often lose sight of their own feelings, ideas, motives, and preferences in the process. Children are vulnerable in relationships when they are primed to give in to others in this way.

Points of View (Session II, E). Pairs of children role-play an argument between parents about a box (made by the leader according to instructions in the manual) that is black on one side, white on the other, and black, white, and gray on the ends. Each "parent" is positioned on one side of the box, so that only the black or the white is visible. One argues that the box is white, the other that it is black. Those watching are the "children." They are positioned to see the ends of the box that are black, white, and also gray. The activity introduces the children to the idea that other perspectives about their parents' conflict are possible.

A Fantasy Room (Session III, A). Children are invited to imagine and then draw a private room that no one else can enter without their permission. The room may be any size, shape, color, or location and may contain whatever the child wishes. The room is a way to represent the self. The walls represent a boundary between the self and others. In subsequent sessions the leader has the option of using guided imagery to help the children enter this inner space in their minds. It becomes a safe place of retreat where the children can identify private thoughts, feelings, or wishes.

The Gift (Session IV, B). The leader guides the children to their "inner room" and suggests that they find a gift there. Once the image is in place, the leader asks them to think about what the gift is, who sent it, and whether there is a message attached. When the children have identified their gift, they can draw a picture of it in their room. This addition, like others that follow, becomes a concrete way of representing the children's expanding sense of self.

The Private Wish (Session V, B). The leader guides the children to their inner room and suggests that they find a blackboard there. Once there, they are to imagine that they write down a private wish on the blackboard. The wish is then written on paper that is placed inside an envelope and taped to the drawing of the imaginary room.

The Mirror (Session VI, B). The children imagine looking into a mirror in their imaginary room. They are asked to notice what they like and do not like about themselves, as well as anything they wish to change now or as they get older. Children can tape their list of written responses to the drawing of the imaginary room.

The Statue (Session VII, B). The children are guided to their imaginary rooms to imagine a statue of how they really feel inside. They also imagine what the statue might do if it came to life. This activity introduces the idea of an inner self and an outer self.

Keys to the Room (Session VIII, B1). The children are introduced to the idea that they can use their private rooms as a retreat when they are no longer in the group. In this activity they practice going to the room in their minds and then leaving it again.

A Wish for Tomorrow (Session VIII, B2). The children are asked to think about themselves as they might be at age 21 and to make a wish for themselves at that age. The wish is written on a piece of paper shaped like an apple seed and "planted" in a paper cup. The cup is taped closed with instructions not to open it until the year that each individual child will reach 21.

Letter to Parents (Session VIII, E). The children work as a group to write a joint letter to all the parents. The content addresses "things that I want you to know about me." All the children sign the letter, which becomes group property. The letter is not actually sent to the parents.

Identity Shields (Session X, B1; for older age-groups only). The identity shield helps the children to consider the kind of person they want to become as they move toward adolescence. The children each receive a piece of poster board with a shield shape that is divided into five sections: two for parents, two for important others, and one for the child's self. The children write or draw symbols of the qualities of each person that they admire and wish to keep as part of their shield. On the outside of the appropriate section, they draw or write the qualities they reject. Finally, the shield shape is cut from the poster board, and the rejected qualities fall away. The shield represents an ideal, or moral compass, that can guide the children as they mature.

4. Dramatizing and Revising Roles, Relationships, and Rules of Moral Conduct

When children role-play their own and other people's parts in a remembered situation, they bring perceptions, thoughts, and feelings (that have shaped their ideas about relationships) back into awareness. When perceptions, thoughts, and feelings are made conscious in this way, they become available for revision.

Rules of Role Play (Session III, B). The leader prompts role-plays with a series of pictures (included in the manual) that suggest situations common in high-conflict families. When these pictures are not relevant, the leader may substitute others or simply allow the children to suggest their own situations. The child who volunteers the role-play situation directs the group members, telling them what feelings, thoughts, and actions go with their individual roles. After each role play, the leader asks the director to develop a revised version that shows how he or she wishes the situation had gone. All the role plays are videotaped by a designated group member. The children review and discuss the videotapes at the end of each session. Directing, role playing, role switching, revising, and video reviewing all provide opportunities for the children to surface and reconsider thoughts and feelings about the reenacted event. In so doing, they gain a measure of distance and mastery.

Role Play of Child Caught Between Parents (Session III, C). This role play evokes children's thoughts and feelings about their role in their parents' conflicts.

Role Play of Child Going Between Houses (Session IV, C). This role play can capture children's thoughts and feelings about going back and forth between their parents. The transitions may refer to visits between different homes, or within the zone of conflict in the same home.

Role Plays About Right and Wrong (Session V, D). This role play is developed in response to a picture of a child watching parents who are fighting. The leader uses the role plays and the revised versions to help the children consider their thoughts and feelings about right and wrong ways for people to treat each other in relationships.

Role Plays of Feelings and Actions (Session VI, D). Children role-play situations in which they or another person had very strong feelings and acted on them in a wrong or unhelpful way. The children create revised role plays to practice alternative methods of conflict resolution.

Masks and Role Plays (Session VII, E). Children role-play situations in which they had to hide their real feelings. In the role play they use actual masks created in *Masks* (Session VII, D) when they are hiding their feelings. At certain points in the role play they remove the masks to tell the camera what they really feel underneath. The leader helps the children to consider when and with whom they feel safe enough to remove their masks.

"Turtle Story" Role Plays (Session X, B2; for younger children). The children reenact "The Turtle Story" (Session X, A), creating their own versions in the process.

5. Defining and Revising Roles, Relationships, and Rules of Moral Conduct

Children who live with conflict tend to develop rigid and sometimes distorted ideas about family roles, relationships, and morality. Activities that address these issues are designed to raise questions about what is right, fair, and expectable in relationships, as well as to surface feelings that are associated with these concerns.

Jobs for People in Your Family (Session V, C). The leader helps the children to define areas of responsibility that are appropriate for children (e.g., learning in school, following the rules) and those that are appropriate for adults (e.g., protecting the children, settling their own fights).

Review of Rules (Session V, E1; for older children). The older children clarify rules of moral conduct as they review the videotape of the role plays about right and wrong that are conducted in Session V.

Review of Jobs (Session V, E2; for younger children). In the review of the videotape of the role plays about right and wrong in Session V, the younger children clarify whether or not the jobs that the role players have taken on are appropriate for them.

How to Act on Feelings (Session VI, C). The leader helps the children to identify right and wrong ways to act on feelings.

Facts About Feelings and Actions (Session VI, E). Leader provides five facts about the differences between feelings and actions.

Family Sculpture (Session VIII, C). The leader helps each group member to form other group members into a human sculpture of his or her family. The sculpture represents the child's view of the way people in his or her family relate to each other most of the time. When the sculpture is completed, it is silently videotaped. The leader then helps each child to identify the ways that the sculpture shows his or her ideas about what is expectable in family relationships.

Fantasy Family Sculpture (Session VIII, D). Each child creates an ideal version of the family sculpture. It is silently videotaped. The sculpture of the ideal family provides the children with an opportunity to review and revise their ideas about relationships and their role in the family. This second part of the exercise can evoke very strong feelings, so the work requires careful monitoring by the leader at every step.

TV Panel of Experts (Session IX, B1; for older children). Children create a panel of experts on family conflict and divorce. The panel is dramatized and videotaped as a television talk show. Members of the panel give advice to children who live with conflict, who send "letters" (prepared by the leader according to the instructions in the manual) to the panel. The activity helps the children to clarify and confirm their own ideas about relationships.

Solving Dilemmas (Session IX, B2; for younger children). Children role-play dilemmas and work together to identify different ways of coping with or solving them.

"The Turtle Story" (Session X, A). The leader reads a story about a sea turtle and a land turtle who loved each other and had sea-land turtle children together. Eventually, though, the adult turtles found that they were so different that it was impossible for them to be happy together. The story provides a way for the children to understand their parents' conflict in a realistic way. The story also introduces the possibility that being a child of two very different people can be an asset rather than a liability.

PLANNING AND MANAGING A GROUP

How should I prepare for each session?

Once the group is under way, it is important for the leader to review the session plans before each meeting and to have a general idea about which activities might be emphasized and which might be minimized or dropped entirely. This judgment will be based on the leader's ability to match the needs of a particular group to the therapeutic goal of the activity. The needs of a particular group can be determined by intake procedures and ongoing experience with the children in session. The therapeutic goal of the activity can be determined by reading Table 1 (check the column heading where the activity appears) as well as by reading the clinical notes provided in the manual within each session. These clinical notes explain the connection between the activity and the therapeutic goal.

Can I change the wording of the instructions to the children in each session?

Yes! The words in the manual are suggestions to help the leader be completely clear about the nature of the activity. It is important, however, for the leader to read the manual and then translate the words to fit the way he or she naturally talks to the children. If this translating does not happen, the group experience will seem stilted and unnatural.

Do I have to include all the activities in every session?

No! In most sessions there will be more activities than time allows. In addition, some activities will generate a lot of discussion and interest, others will not. The leader will need to have an idea about which activities seem most relevant as well as their place in the whole sequence of the group approach. With these considerations in mind, the leader can decide what to spend time on and what to drop.

What if the children are acting out?

Refer to Appendix A, Troubleshooting.

Do I have to give snack?

Snack is one way to help these children to feel nurtured and safe. Snack works best when the food is not brought to the room until snack time and when it is available in unlimited quantities (e.g., popcorn) or in specified quantities (e.g., two cookies each, no more, no less).

What if I am having a hard time understanding the children and their treatment needs?

For a more complete discussion of children who live in highly conflicted or violent families, as well as the theoretical rationale for this treatment approach, we recommend the companion volume to this manual: *In the Name of the Child: A Developmental Approach to Understanding and Helping Children of Conflicted and Violent Divorce* (Johnston & Roseby, Free Press, New York, 1997).

What if 10 sessions are not enough?

For some children, particularly those in the general divorcing population, group treatment plus additional work with parents will provide adequate support. Others benefit from being able to participate in more than 10 sessions. Because each session in this manual details a very full agenda, leaders may decide to extend the number of sessions; all together, there is enough material for 20 or more sessions. Some leaders have evolved ongoing groups that periodically graduate old members and admit new ones. Some children benefit from cycling through two or three different 10-session groups. Finally, some children are more able to feel comfortable in individual counseling after their experience in group treatment.

TABLE 1

SEQUENCE OF MAIN GROUP ACTIVITIES AND THEIR THERAPEUTIC GOALS

Session	Creating Common Ground & Safety	Exploring the Language & Complexity of Feelings	Defining & Understanding the Self	Roles, Relationships, & Rules	
				Dramatizing/Revising	Defining/Revising
I.	*(B) Rules (C) House My Family Lives In	(D) List of Feelings (E) Feelings/Color			
II.	(B) Blind Walk	(C) Level of Feelings (D) Charade of Feelings	(E) Points of View		
III.	(A) Relaxation		(A) A Fantasy Room	(B) Rules of Role Play (C) Role Play of Child Caught Between Parents	
IV.	(A) Relaxation		(B) The Gift (with optional visualization)	(C) Role Play of Child Going Between Houses	
V.	(A) Relaxation		(B) The Private Wish (with optional visualization)	(D) Role Plays About Right and Wrong	(C) Jobs for People In Your Family (E1) Review of Rules (E2) Review of Jobs
VI.	(A) Relaxation		(B) The Mirror (with optional visualization)	(D) Role Plays of Feelings and Action	(C) How to Act on Feelings (E) Facts About Feelings and Actions
VII.	(A) Relaxation	(C) Inside Me/Outside Me (D) Masks	(B) The Statue (with optional visualization)	(E) Masks and Role Plays	
VIII.	(A) Relaxation		(B1) Keys to the Room (B2) A Wish for Tomorrow (with optional visualization) (E) Letter to Parents		(C) Family Sculpture (D) Fantasy Family Sculpture
IX.	(A) Group Art Project				
X.			(B1) Identity Shields	(B2) "TheTurtle Story" Role Plays	(B1) TV Panel of Experts (B2) Solving Dilemmas (A) "The Turtle Story"

*Letters correspond to the sequence of the activity as it is labeled in each session in the manual.

SESSION I

SAYING HELLO AND MAKING A SAFE PLACE TO WORK TOGETHER

GOALS

1. To create common ground and safety.

2. To help children to identify a range of feelings that they may have experienced in response to family violence or conflict

NOTE TO LEADER: Save all work generated during the group time. Be sure that it is clearly labeled. Keep each child's work in a separate folder that can be reviewed with the child in an individual follow-up session and selectively with parents when the child permits.

MATERIALS

NOTE TO LEADER: Materials starred with an asterisk are reproduced in the manual at the end of the session.

1. Polaroid camera and film (optional).

2. Folder for each child in the group.

3. 3x5 cards folded in half.

4. Plenty of paper, pencils, markers, and rulers.

5. A poster board for rules (see Section B of this session). After it is made, display this chart in every session.

6. Large sheets of blank paper.

*7. List of Feelings.

PROCEDURE

A. Introduction

CLINICAL NOTE: Emphasis is on creating a sense of common ground and safety.

Leader introduces self and asks the group members to say their names. Then leader says in his or her own words:

> I'm so glad you all were able to come today. I'm really looking forward to us getting to know each other, doing some work, as well as having some fun together. In case you didn't know, I'd like to tell you right away that all of you share something in common. You have all had experience with fighting in your families that can be frightening and hard to live with. [Add if appropriate] Some of you have parents who live apart, and some of you do not. [Or add if appropriate] You also all have parents who don't live together because they are separated or divorced.

The leader goes around the table in order and has children say their names and tell something about themselves that makes them different from everyone else in their family. The leader asks the children to fill in their names on the folded 3x5 cards in front of them, then to write or draw their response to the question on the card. If a Polaroid camera is available, the leader can now take a picture of each child and attach it to the name card. Leader then says in his or her own words:

> At the end of group, I will collect the name tags you made today. I will set them out at the beginning of group next time. That will mark your place to sit in group. It will stay the same for the whole time. If you are absent, we will have your name tag to keep your special place.

A leader who has had individual intake sessions with all the children can comment in his or her own words:

> I have met you all separately, and you and I have shared some things about your family situation that you may or may not want to share with the group. That's your decision to make.

Leader then continues in his or her own words, regarding confidentiality:

> If something comes up during the group and any of you find you'd like to talk with me privately, please let me know. Please don't talk to other kids about

what goes on here. It's important for us all to feel safe and private, so that we can tell what we want to tell and keep things private when we want to. It is up to you, though, whether or not you talk to your parents about group. As most of you know, I will be working with your parents also. I will try to help them understand you, but I will not tell them exact things you say or show them any work you do without your permission.

We will be meeting every week for the next [specify number] weeks. We will all be here to help each other. Each time we meet we will do four things:

1. We will do some relaxation exercises to help us get calmed down.

2. We will do some activity to get to know each other and ourselves better.

3. We will do some role-playing, which we will videotape.

4. We will watch ourselves on video and eat a snack.

You will each have a chance to be in charge of the role plays and to watch others role-playing as well. Everyone will also have a turn to be the camera person. Let's decide now on the order for taking turns as camera person.

Leader helps group determine a sequence for camera duty that gives a fair share of time to each group member. Leader then asks for questions and points of clarification, and generally checks in with the group to reflect and clarify feelings that children may be communicating nonverbally. Leader may wish to model identification and expression of feelings by sharing his or her own feelings about the group.

B. Rules (To be posted at each session)

CLINICAL NOTE: Emphasis is on communicating real concern for the children's sense of safety in the group.

Leader says in his or her own words:

Let's think of three or four simple rules for the group that will help us all feel safe.

The leader tries to get children to come up with and agree on rules. If necessary, the leader facilitates by suggesting the rules listed below. The group should end up with some variant of the rules below plus one or two additional rules. The leader writes them on the chart. This chart will be displayed at every session.

1. Only one person speaks at a time.

2. Listen when another person is talking.

3. No gossiping outside of group (that includes leader).

4. No put-downs.

C. House My Family Lives In

CLINICAL NOTE: Emphasis is on identifying similarities that create common ground as well as supporting differences in feelings and family structures.

Leader says in his or her own words:

> Now that we have some rules, let's take some time to show each other who are the different people in our family and where they live. Think first about who are the people that you think are part of your family. You might want to include your mother, father, brothers, sisters, grandparents, or special friends. Remember, group is a safe place for you and your ideas. There may be people who are not really in your family, but you think they are, so you can include them if you like. There might be other people who think they're in your family, but you don't feel that way about them, so you can leave them out or draw them on the back if you like. Then think about where everyone lives.

Leader may model by drawing the houses or apartments where members of his or her immediate or extended family live. Group members begin working as soon as they understand the task. Very anxious/vigilant children may wish to use rulers. After the drawings are finished, each child may share his or her drawing and name family members. Leader follows each child's presentation with one or two of these questions:

1. Do you go back and forth between your mother's and your father's houses, or between their fights at home?

2. Is that hard?

3. What is hard about that?

4. What is fun about that?

5. Do you ever wish you could live with someone else or spend more time with someone else in your family?

6. Do you sometimes wish that someone in your family was not there? [OR] Who would you like to have in your family?

(The following additional questions are for younger children only.)

7. Is someone still in your family if they go and live in a different house?

8. Can you love someone who lives in a different house just as much as someone who lives with you?

D. List of Feelings

CLINICAL NOTE: Emphasis is on helping the children to identify as wide a range of feelings as possible, and creating an encouraging and accepting atmosphere. It is also important to introduce the notion of mixed and complex feelings.

Leader provides some type of verbal transition and closure from previous activity, then says in his or her own words:

I'd like us to do something together that other groups have done with me before. We all had a lot of fun. What we did was to make a list of all the different feelings that group members had about the fighting and arguing that has gone on in their families. Kids came up with all kinds of feelings—mad, bad, sad, scared, and so on. I have an old list here from a group I had before [see Materials section for this session]. I'd like us to make our own list together, and we'll see if you can get as many feelings on your list as there are on my old list. Maybe you can get even more. I'll write, and you can just tell me what to put on our list.

As the list is being compiled, leader continually encourages a wide range of feelings and the possibility of outdoing the old list (see List of Feelings, p. 22). When the new list is done, the group compares lists. Children like to count the number of feelings in the old list and the new list. When counting is done, compare. Children can add from the old list to their list as well as cross out items on the old list that they don't like. When the comparing, adding, and crossing out are done, the leader creates some closure by commenting on the range of feelings and noting how some feelings are easier to talk about than others, how feelings vary from time to time, and how feelings mix together.

E. Feelings/Color

In this activity, the leader helps the children to create a color-coded chart on which feelings that have been identified are associated with a particular color or combination of colors. For example, "angry" may be red, whereas "embarrassed" may be red combined with other colors because it has an anger component. Other colors in the combination should reflect the other feeling components. The group should decide on each color or color combination by consensus as much as possible.

Leader should decide, if there is disagreement. Once the color or color combination is chosen, the feelings word should be circled in that color(s) on the feelings chart. It is not necessary to spend huge amounts of time on each decision. The finished chart is the point. It will be a useful tool in future sessions.

F. Closure, Snack, and Housekeeping

CLINICAL NOTE: Emphasis is on creating a sense of order, continuity, and safekeeping.

During snack, the leader collects name tags, stressing that they will be put out at the next group meeting. The leader collects any artwork that the children have done and makes sure that the work has the child's name on it. The leader places the work in the child's folder and reassures the group that their work will be kept safely for them until next time. The leader reviews the name of the camera person for next week and reminds that child to come 15 minutes early to practice with the video camera.

List of Feelings
(Materials—Session I)

Angry	Mad
Frustrated	Upset
Depressed	Hateful
Hated	Shy
Afraid	Pressured
Worried	Confused
Sad	Left Out
Fidgety	Guilty
Jealous	Scared
Helpless	Embarrassed

SESSION II

EXPLORING LEVELS OF FEELINGS, ACTIONS, AND POINTS OF VIEW

GOALS

1. To create common ground and safety

2. To help the children to become aware that feelings can be experienced at different levels of intensity

3. To help the children to understand the difference between feelings and actions

4. To introduce the idea of right and wrong ways to act on feelings

5. To help the children to define their own perspective on the family conflict

MATERIALS

NOTE TO LEADER: Materials starred with an asterisk are reproduced in the manual at the end of the session.

1. Video camera and monitor.

2. Rules chart (posted in group room).

3. Feelings/Color Chart developed in Session I (posted in group room).

4. Name tags and folders (to be kept in leader's possession and placed around the table before each session).

5. Plenty of paper, pencils, markers, and rulers.

6. Blindfold.

*7.   **Feelings Measure Chart.**

*8.   **Shoe box (or larger box).**

PROCEDURE

A. Introduction

The leader goes around the table and makes a brief statement of welcome. The leader reminds the children who the camera person is according to the sequence determined during closure in Session I. The leader briefly reviews the rules that were agreed upon in Session I and listed on the posted chart.

> NOTE ON TIMING: The following activity can take up most of the session. The leader can solve this problem by using the same obstacle course for each blind walker and using a timer with a loud bell. The leader then allocates 3–5 minutes per blind walker. When the bell goes off, the course ends wherever the blind walker happens to be.

B. Blind Walk

> CLINICAL NOTE: Emphasis is to create trust within the group and allow children to experience some dependency on peers. It is vital that the walk be conducted safely. Leader should point out how important it is to be able to have help from friends, and note how good it can feel. Each guide and blindfolded follower should be applauded when they reach "home" or the end of their allotted time. Each should be complimented, one for being such a good caretaker and the other for taking a big chance and being brave.

For Blind Walk activity, the group is directed to create an obstacle course through which each group member will be guided while blindfolded.

1.   A volunteer is identified (or selected) and blindfolded so that he or she does not see the course as it is being created. *Reassurance from the leader here is both necessary and appropriate.*

2.   Each group member is then given an area and instructed to create an obstacle for the course (each obstacle to be connected to the obstacles on either side). The creator of an obstacle has the responsibility of guiding the blindfolded child safely through his or her part of the obstacle course. *For older children or mixed-gender groups, verbal directions may have to replace physical contact between group members.*

3   The leader oversees the course to make sure it is connected and safe.

4.   If there is time, the obstacles in the course are changed after each blind walker is identified and blindfolded. The process is repeated until each group member has gone through the course blindfolded.

C. Level of Feelings

CLINICAL NOTE: Focus of this exercise is to make feelings seem less uncontrollable by introducing the idea that feelings may be experienced at different levels rather than in all-or-nothing extremes.

The leader passes out copies of the Feelings Measure Chart (see Materials section) to each child and goes over the feelings that are labeled under the first three measures. The leader explains that other children whose parents are fighting, separated, or divorced sometimes have these feelings. The leader asks the children to fill in how strongly they have felt these three feelings in their own lives. Leader says in his or her own words:

> Now pick two, three, or four other feelings that are most true for you and write them in under the other four measures on your chart. You can use the Feelings/Color chart to help you if you like. After you have filled in the name of each feeling, decide how strongly you feel this way and fill that in too.

When the exercise is completed, the leader invites each group member to share what he or she has done. Prompt questions about feelings should be selected by the leader from the following:

> What do you usually do when you feel [fill in a feeling]?
>
> Do you ever feel——in a different amount?
>
> What do you do then and how is that different?
>
> What makes you feel——?
>
> When you feel extremely——, what can make you feel different?
>
> How about when you feel just a little——?

D. Charade of Feelings

CLINICAL NOTE: This activity introduces role playing and the idea that different levels of feelings are acted on in different ways. Again the point is to make feelings seem less uncontrollable.

The leader says in his or her own words:

> Now that we have had a chance to talk about feelings a little, I would like us to get ready to do some role playing. We'll start with charades. Who can tell me what charades are?

Seek and then summarize response. Then leader says in his or her own words:

> OK, let's start out simply. The charades will help us to role-play our feelings and think about how people might show a little bit of a feeling instead of a lot of that feeling. I would like each of you to pick one feeling from your chart and then get ready to charade the feeling. It will be our job to guess the feeling and how much you are feeling it.

Leader goes around the table giving each group member a turn. Passing is OK, but leader should gently press by saying, for example:

> Could you charade a person sleeping or feeling nothing? Would that be OK?

It is very important to go gently and respectfully, being alert to the need to back off quickly if the child is obviously uncomfortable. Go around the table once or twice, as long as the group is focused.

E. Points of View

NOTE ON TIMING: There may be very little time left for this activity after the Blind Walk. This activity requires at least 20 minutes. If there is not enough time to complete it in this session, introduce it in Session III after the fantasy and relaxation exercises.

CLINICAL NOTE: Focus of this activity is to help the children to gain some distance and perspective on the family conflict.

For the Points of View activity, a shoe box (see Materials section) is placed in the center of the group table, in such a way that only the black side can be seen from one side of the room, only the white side can be seen from the other side of the room, and the black, gray, and white sides can be seen only from one side or another. Leader may need to raise box (put it on books, etc.) in order to achieve these perspectives. Leader says in his or her own words:

> Let's do something now with this box. Believe it or not, this box is going to

help us understand a bit about grown-up fights. Let's do a little role play using this box.

Leader selects or asks for three volunteers, one for "Mom," one for "Dad," and one for "Child" (both boys and girls may play either of these three roles if they are comfortable doing so). The other group members will have the job of watching the role play and giving advice to the Child. Leader directs Dad to stand on one side of the table (so he can see only the black side of the box). Mom is to stand on the other side of the table (so she can see only the white side of the box), and the Child is to stand to the side (where she or he can see the tricolored side). Leader then asks Dad to describe what he sees to Mom. Focus on eliciting the color. Prompts include:

> How do you feel?
>
> A lot or a little?

Then leader asks Mom to describe what she sees to Dad. Focus on eliciting the color.

> How does Mom feel now? How much?
>
> How does Dad feel now? How much?
>
> How is Child beginning to feel?

Leader facilitates the exercise as it becomes a fight over black and white. Prompts include eliciting feelings of all players as fight escalates. Child's role is to observe. In this exercise it is important to rotate players from position to position, eliciting and noticing changes in feelings as points of view change. Prompts include:

> How did you feel as Dad [as Mom, as Child]?
>
> How did feelings change when you saw the gray side?

Changes could be in feelings or degree of feeling. After the fight has escalated and both parents are very angry, leader elicits from Child what he or she sees.

> What do you see? How come Mom can't see what you see? How come Dad can't see what you see? What is this like for you?

> CLINICAL NOTE: Here the focus is on helping the child to see that there is some black (Dad is partly right), some white (Mom is partly right), and some gray (both right, both wrong).

Leader says in his or her own words:

When you see both sides, it's very confusing and frustrating! Some kids find it easier to see only black or only white. Other kids prefer not to look at all. What can kids do in a situation like this?

Discussion should emphasize that parents won't see things differently if they don't want to; that it's not possible for the child to make them move or see differently, so the child's choices are *(Try to elicit from observers):*

Keep trying to move them. (Leader notes that this can be exhausting, impossible, too hard.)

Understand there is no solution. They can argue about black and white forever.

Child can try to figure out who's right and wrong. Notice that both are right, but both are failing to see the gray, so don't waste too much time on figuring it out.

Child can stay and watch and worry, or try to figure it out. (Leader notes that this can be exhausting and that it takes up lots of time. Leader elicits other age-appropriate activities from group—such as roller skating, homework, biking, reading—which child could be spending time on.)

If time permits, all group members should participate and rotate at least once.

F. Closure, Snack, and Housekeeping

The leader distributes snack, and has group members label and put away any drawings, name cards, etc. The leader reviews the name of the camera person for next week and reminds that child to come 15 minutes early.

Feelings Measure Chart

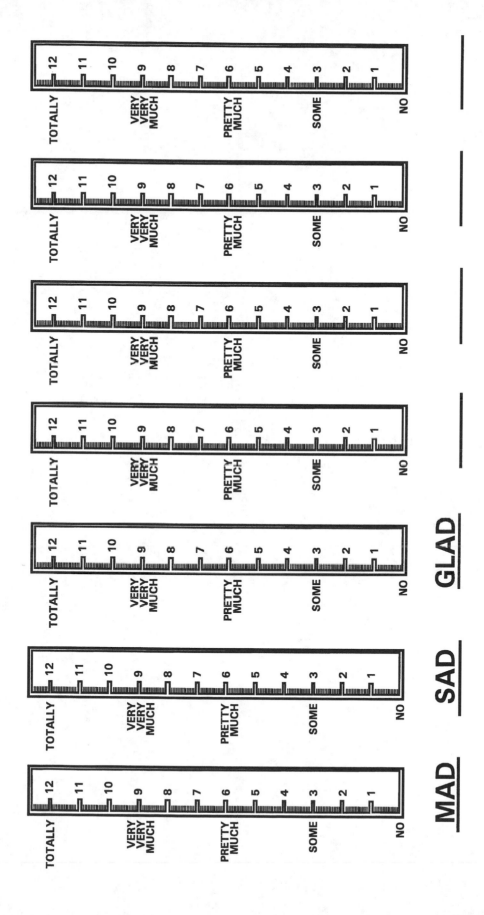

Instructions for Points of View Box

Materials needed:
Black, gray, and white paper
Scissors
Shoe box
Glue

  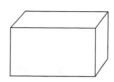

1. Cover top of box, starting on the left side, with gray paper so that the gray paper hangs over the left and right sides of box. Glue it down onto the box.

2. Using white paper, cover front of box, starting at the bottom, and overlap gray paper on top of box about 1/3 in from top front edge.

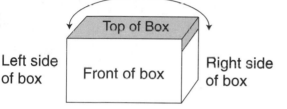

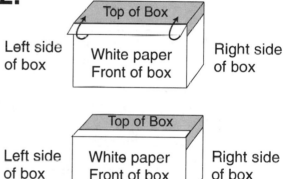

3. Using black paper, cover back of box, starting at the bottom, and overlap gray paper on top of box about 1/3 in from top back edge.

4.   Finished Box

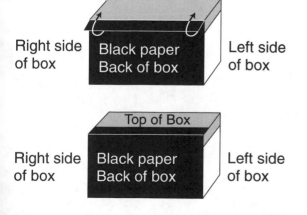

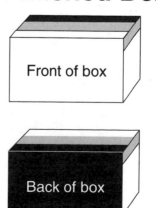

SESSION III

MAKING A SAFE INSIDE PLACE AND LEARNING THE RULES OF ROLE PLAY

GOALS

1. To help the children to define and understand themselves by introducing the idea of a safe inner space

2. To teach the way role playing will be done in group

3. To help the children to dramatize their own experience of being caught in the family conflict so their thoughts and feelings can be identified, fantasies and wishes can be clarified and reality-tested, and issues of right and wrong can be discussed.

MATERIALS

NOTE TO LEADER: Materials starred with an asterisk are reproduced in the manual at the end of the session.

1. Video camera and monitor.

2. Rules chart (posted in group room).

3. Feelings/Color Chart developed in Session I (posted in group room).

4. Name tags and folders (to be kept in leader's possession).

5. Plenty of paper, pencils, markers, and rulers.

*6. Picture of Child Caught Between Two Parents.

Procedure

A. A Fantasy Room

CLINICAL NOTE: This exercise is a concrete way to help the children to think about themselves and their boundaries. The room that is created will be used in subsequent sessions to help children to visualize a private place to be in during relaxation exercises.

The leader says a brief word of welcome to the group in general and acknowledges each child individually while distributing name tags and noting who will be the camera person today. Leader says in his or her own words:

> Today we're going to spend about 10 minutes on ourselves. Let me tell you why I think it's important to do this. Sometimes when families/parents fight, I have noticed that kids spend a lot of time thinking about the fighting. Some kids worry about it.

The leader makes reference here to the Feelings/Color Chart.

> As you see from this list, other kids feel ——————or——————[fill in blanks with feelings that suggest worry or avoidance].

The leader notes ways in which such feelings focus children's attention away from their own needs. Leader says in his or her own words:

> Now it does seem that that's a lot of work, and it makes it hard, sometimes, to think about who you are as a -year-old person: what you think, what you feel, what you like and don't like. So in this session, let's just take about 10 minutes to think about these things. I'm going to give you some paper, and I want you to have fun drawing your very own room. No one may enter this room but you, unless you decide to invite someone in. No one at all. It is completely your own.

The leader distributes drawing paper and continues:

> You can draw your room with or without a lock, with or without windows. It can be large or small. Underground, above ground, or in the sky. It can be any color and, best of all, it can have anything in it you like. Anything at all. Go as far as your imagination will carry you.

While group is working, the leader comments supportively about each drawing and asks the children to try to stay relaxed. The leader allows about 10 minutes for this activity, then brings the activity to a close and asks each group member if he or she would like to share their drawing.

B. Rules of Role Play

CLINICAL NOTE: Emphasis is on empowering the director and helping children become aware that different feelings are associated with different roles, that some feelings are easily shown while others are not, and that feelings vary in level or intensity.

The leader is now ready to introduce role playing, which will be conducted according to the following rules. The leader should review the rules listed below prior to the group and then paraphrase them to the group members at this time.

1. Ideas for role plays come from the children whenever possible.

2. The child who makes up the role play has the choice of being the director. The director picks who plays what role, reminds the group of the story, and directs what they say, how they say it, and what movement is appropriate. The leader facilitates and supports the director. It is important, before the role play begins, to help the director to identify a feeling for each role and how the feeling is to be shown or hidden. The possibility of mixed or ambivalent feelings should be suggested when appropriate and whenever possible.

3. If the child who offers the role play chooses not to be the director, he or she may select a role to play and may choose another director.

4. Children may negotiate for a different role when picked or, if the child prefers no role, he or she is included in the role of houseplant, family pet, etc. This is true even for the child who offered the role play. This way no child stays completely out of the role play.

5. All role plays are videotaped by the camera person for the week. Videotapes are reviewed at the end of the session.

6. In theory, all group members should have a chance to take each role. In practice, the group will probably get to do the role play about three times, with different children in different roles each time.

C. Role Play of Child Caught Between Parents

CLINICAL NOTE: Focus is on helping the child to identify the feelings she or he has when caught in the middle, differentiate these feelings from the feelings of the parents in the conflict situation, identify fantasies and wishes, and engage in reality testing.

The leader shows the picture of Child Caught Between Two Parents (see Materials section) to the group and says in his or her own words:

> What is happening here? What do you think the child is feeling? What do you think each adult is feeling? Did anything like this ever happen to you, so that, if you pleased your mom, you upset your dad; or if you pleased your dad, you got your mom upset or mad? Draw a little cartoon or picture of what happened. Think about where it happened, who said what, etc. Then take the colored markers and color all the feelings everyone had in the scene [using the Feelings/Color Chart as a guide].

The leader asks if one of the children who self-discloses would like to direct a role play. Work proceeds according to the rules described above. During and/or after each role play the leader should help the role players to generate as many different feelings as possible. The leader gives lots of encouragement for discriminating between feelings, differentiating people's feelings, and discriminating levels of feeling. The leader may model responses. If children have difficulty in identifying feelings, use the Feelings/Color Chart as a prompt. Also, leader helps children to discriminate how much of each feeling they have in the role play (totally, pretty much, etc.) as on the Feelings Measure Chart from Session II. Leader must restore the child's "face" if she or he reveals weakness, pain, or embarrassment. The leader may say, for example:

> [Child's name] was really very brave/very honest, when he [she] said "[quote the child]"

Then it is useful to point out the "no-win" situation:

> Sometimes, if you obey your mom, you disobey your dad (and vice versa).

> CLINICAL NOTE: Validate all feelings. Emphasize that feelings are never wrong, that it's what you do with feelings in action that can be right or wrong, and that different people can have different or similar feelings about the same event (using differences among group members as examples).

To counter the feelings of helplessness, blame, or shame, etc., the leader can encourage fantasies of what children would like to have happened during the role play. For example, at the end of a role play, the leader can say in his or her own words:

> How would you like to have intervened/acted? Pretend that you are all-pow-erful or magic; what would you do? Let's do the role play that way.

During and after the role play, the leader notes the realities of the situation and the constraints on the children. The leader says in his or her own words:

> Do you think [the fantasy] might happen? No! I agree, it won't. [If the child has expressed fears, add the following] It was a good idea not to [say any-thing]. You were afraid you'd only make them madder if you did.

The leader validates that they were in a very difficult situation and that they were very brave or wise or did all they could at the time. Leader may point out that it's unfair to children when they are put in these situations.

D. Review and Snack

During snack time, the videotaped role plays are reviewed. Again, emphasis is on eliciting the feelings of the child and differentiating them from the feelings of the parents in the conflict situation. Closure questions on this include the following points:

> Do you think what is happening is fair?
>
> What do the parents want the child to do?
>
> What does the child wish he/she could do?
>
> What can a child do?
>
> What would you like to do if you become a parent?
>
> What sometimes makes it hard for parents to do the right thing?

E. Closure and Housekeeping

The leader collects and labels all drawings from the session and stores them in the children's folders. Leader collects name tags and designates a camera person for the next session.

Child Caught Between Two Parents

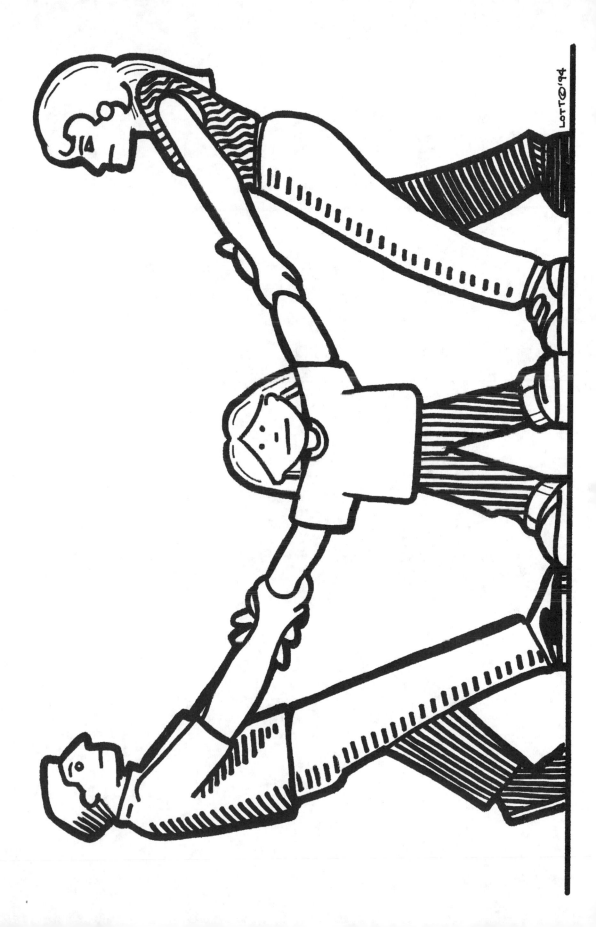

SESSION IV

EXPLORING A SAFE INSIDE PLACE AND BACK TO REALITY
Role Playing Going Back and Forth Between Parents Who Fight

GOALS

1. To help the children to explore private hopes and wishes in a safe inner place

2. To help the children to identify feelings and thoughts when they go back and forth between parents in the zone of conflict

MATERIALS

NOTE TO LEADER: Materials starred with an asterisk are reproduced in the manual at the end of the session.

1. Video camera and monitor.

2. Rules chart (posted in group room).

3. Feelings/Color Chart developed in Session I (posted in group room).

4. Name tags and folders (to be kept in leader's possession).

5. Plenty of paper, pencils, markers, and rulers.

6. Construction paper folded to look like a gift card, one piece for each child (plus extras for mistakes).

*7. Picture of Child Going Between Two Houses.

PROCEDURE

A. Relaxation

CLINICAL NOTE: The focus of these relaxation exercises is on awareness and mastery of physical tension states. For younger or less
mature groups, these introductory activities can be done without the
guided visualization. Separate instructions are given below for
groups that are visualizing before drawing and for groups that are
drawing only.

The leader goes around the table and makes a brief statement of welcome. The
leader reminds the group who the camera person is for that day. Then the leader
says in his or her own words:

> Remember, in the last session you were learning to relax a little. Let's see how
> many of you have your shoulders attached to your earlobes right now.
> [Leader demonstrates with tense shoulders.] Let's try to get these shoulders
> relaxed. I will count down from 10 to 0. You can close your eyes if you like.

B. The Gift. *For groups that are visualizing, instructions begin here. For groups that are drawing only, go directly to B1 below.*

Leader says in his or her own words:

> With your eyes still closed, I want you to imagine the door to your special pri-
> vate room. Can you see it? Open it and look around. Notice if the room you
> drew has changed at all. Is it the same? [Pause] Different? [Pause] Now imag-
> ine that a gift to you has appeared in your private room, which you drew last
> week. You walk over to it. Is it large? Small? Open your gift. It is special, exact-
> ly what you want. Enjoy it for a few minutes. [Pause] There is a card attached
> to your gift. Read it. [Pause] What does it say? Does it say who your gift is
> from? [Pause] Now decide if you wish to leave it in the room or bring it out.
> [Pause] Now I will count back down from 10 to 0. At 10 you will begin to leave
> your room and slowly come back to the group, and arrive back here at 0.

Leader counts slowly back from 10 to 0, then says in his or her own words:

> Now, while we're still relaxed, I want you to take a few minutes to draw your
> gift into the picture of the room. You can draw on a separate sheet of paper
> and attach it to your room if you like. After you have done this, write down,
> in private, what the gift card says.

The leader distributes folded paper for the gift card message. The leader invites but does not press group members to share when they have finished the activity.

B1. The Gift. *For groups that are drawing only, instructions begin here.*

Leader says in his or her own words:

> I want you to imagine that a gift to you has appeared in your private room, which you drew last week. The gift is really special, something that you really want. Try to decide what it is. Also there is a card attached. Try to decide who the gift is from and what the card says. Now take a few minutes and draw your gift into the drawing of your room. You can draw on a separate sheet of paper and then attach it to your room if you like. Then write down what your gift card says. Attach that to your room also.

The leader distributes extra paper as needed for the gift drawing and folded paper for the gift card message. The leader invites but does not press group members to share when they have finished the activity.

C. Role Play of Child Going Between Houses

The leader says in his or her own words:

> Last time we talked about how it feels to be caught in the middle of our parents, to be pulled in two. Sometimes the feeling of being caught like that comes up when you go back and forth between your parents. Some of them live in separate houses, and some don't; either way it can be hard going back and forth in an angry space between parents. Even when you love them both, you may have a lot of different feelings. Take a look at this picture [see Child Going Between Two Houses]. Can you think of a time when something happened that you didn't like, or maybe just didn't understand, when you were going between parents? Think of that time now. Who would like to direct a role play about that?

Videotape the role play. During the role plays, leader focuses on eliciting the feelings of the child toward the parents. When role plays are done, leader may ask in his or her own words:

> Do parents sometimes act in ways that are hard to understand? Would it help if parents explained what they were feeling and who they are upset with (if

they are upset) and why? Is there another way that parents could handle their relationship and the space between them that would make it easier for the child?

If there is time, the leader helps the children to develop a role play around an alternative way of going back and forth in the space between parents.

D. Review and Snack

During snack, the role plays are reviewed on the monitor. The leader talks about the connections between feelings and behavior at transitions (e.g., "Sometimes when you come home to your mom, you kind of miss your dad and you feel sad or irritable." Or, "Sometimes it feels like the divorce is happening all over again when you see your dad drive off." Or, "When you hear your dad say 'not nice' things about your mom, it sometimes kind of hurts inside"). The leader asks if anyone has figured out a way to feel better about going back and forth.

E. Closure and Housekeeping

The leader collects name tags and any artwork that the children produced. The leader makes sure that the work has the child's name on it, then places it in the appropriate folder. The leader identifies the camera person for the next session.

SESSION V

DEFINING WISHES FOR YOURSELF AND RULES THAT WORK FOR YOUR FAMILY AND RELATIONSHIPS

GOALS

1. To clarify roles and boundaries in families

2. To help the children to dramatize specific conflict situations so that their thoughts and feelings can be identified, fantasies and wishes can be clarified and reality-tested, and issues of right and wrong can be discussed

3. To help the children to construct a code of ethics or rules for relationships

MATERIALS

NOTE TO LEADER: Materials starred with an asterisk are reproduced in the manual at the end of the session.

1. Video camera and monitor.

2. Rules chart (posted in group room).

3. Feelings/Color Chart developed in Session I (posted in group room).

4. Name tags and folders (to be kept in leader's possession).

5. Plenty of paper, pencils, markers, and rulers.

6. Envelopes and tape for groups who are not doing visualization during relaxation.

*7. Picture of Child Watching Parents Fight.

8. Flip chart and markers.

PROCEDURE

A. Relaxation

The leader goes around the table and makes a brief statement of welcome. The leader reminds the group of who the camera person is for that day.

The leader says in his or her own words:

> Let's check in and see how tense or relaxed we all are. Check your shoulders. Scrunch them up tight, then let them flop. Again. Now let's check arms. Make a fist and hold your arm out tightly in front of you. Now relax; let your arm get heavy and fall. Again. OK. Now I will count down from 10 to 0, so that you can spend a little time in your own space. You can close your eyes if you like.

B. The Private Wish. *For groups that are visualizing, instructions begin here. For groups that are drawing only, go directly to B1 below.*

The leader counts down slowly, then says in his or her own words:

> With your eyes still closed, I want you to imagine the door to your special private room. Can you see it? Is it the same? [Pause] Is it different? [Pause] Now go in and look around. Is it the same this week? [Pause] Any changes? [Pause] Now imagine that on one wall there is a very large blackboard that you have never noticed before. [Pause] Can you see it? [Pause] There is chalk and an eraser. You walk up to it. [Pause] Touch the board. [Pause] Pick up the chalk. [Pause] Now imagine that you are writing one thing you wish or think (maybe about someone or something in your family) but never say out loud. [Long pause] It can be any wish at all that is yours and yours alone. I will not ask you to write it down or share it when we're done, unless you want to. [Pause again] Now decide if you wish to erase your message or leave it on the board. [Pause] Now I will count back up from 0 to 10. At 0 you will begin to leave your room and slowly come back to the group, and arrive at 10.

Leader then counts slowly from 0 to 10.

Children are then asked to add a blackboard to their drawing of the room and to write their three private wishes on that blackboard; or they may use a separate sheet of paper, insert it into an envelope, and attach it to their drawing of the room. The leader invites but does not press for sharing, and then moves on to the next activity.

B1. The Private Wish. *For groups that are drawing only, instructions begin here:*

Leader asks the children to add a blackboard to their drawing of their room. The leader then asks them to write down on a piece of paper three private wishes that they would write on their blackboard. The leader explains that these may be wishes that they haven't told anyone, maybe haven't felt safe telling anyone. The leader explains further that, in order to keep the wishes private, they are to place them in a envelope and then seal and tape the envelope at the end of the activity. The leader invites but does not press for sharing, and then moves on to the next activity.

C. Jobs for People in Your Family

CLINICAL NOTE: Emphasis here is on clarifying appropriate role boundaries and areas of responsibility within families.

The leader has the children sit around the table (in front of the flip chart) to generate a list of what are kids' jobs, rights, and responsibilities in a family and what are parents' jobs, rights, and responsibilities. The leader writes all suggestions on the chart, and may want to cluster them into appropriate areas for later general classification (example follows):

JOBS CHART

PARENTS	KIDS
Outside-Home Jobs Go to work, earn money	*Outside-Home Jobs* Go to school, get good grades, be a good team member
Child-Rearing/Caring for One Another Jobs Love and protect kids, discipline kids, stop fights	*At-Home Jobs* Do chores, obey parents, love parents, be nice to brother/sister
Inside-Home Jobs Cook food, do household chores, yard work, washing, etc.	*For Self* Relax and watch TV, play alone, play with friends
Self-Care Jobs Enjoy self, relax, see friends, party, date	

The leader also tries to have the children generate rules for the ways people should treat one another generally (especially peers, siblings, and parents): Be polite, kind, gentle; don't hit, push, shove; no put-downs; listen to others; keep an open mind; don't interrupt; take turns or share; etc. (It is not necessary to push the children too far in generating this list because, during the role plays that follow, they will be adding new ones.)

D. Role Plays About Right and Wrong

CLINICAL NOTE: Focus is on developing and affirming codes of moral conduct in relationships.

The leader either presents the stimulus picture (Child Watching Parents Fight) or has the children recall and talk about an argument or fight someone had in their family and/or among their peers. (It is useful to ask for one example from home and one from school.) This can be a specific example or a composite script of what often happens. The leader helps the children to discuss the details and then has the group produce a role play of the situation (using a director, camera person, and actors as developed in previous sessions).

CLINICAL NOTE: It may be useful to consider whether the children can realistically do anything about the fighting or whether it is simply better for the children to make a promise to themselves that they will live by different rules when they get older.

The leader can ask in his or her own words:

In the family that you would like to have, how would you like to treat your husband/wife/children? How would you like them to treat you?

The leader discusses the details of the amended situation and, if appropriate, helps the children to develop a second role play of that situation. The leader repeats the above cycle, leaving about 20 minutes for section E1. or E2. below.

E1. Review of Rules and Snack (For older children)

CLINICAL NOTE: Focus is to help the children to clarify and revise principles of moral conduct in relationships.

While the older children are eating snack, the role plays are reviewed on the monitor. It is the leader's task to frame the specific moral dilemma for the child in that situation: "What should the child do, and why?" The leader helps to tease out the different implications for each family member for the various solutions. The product of this discussion is the elaboration of principles for what is fair, right, proper, unfair, wrong, and improper and under what conditions. These principles should be recorded on the flip chart and elaborated when further group discussions clarify them. Examples:

a. It is never OK for parents to hit one another.

b. It is OK to keep a secret from one's parent if it is not his/her business.

c. It is not fair for kids to have to take sides.

d. It's OK for a kid to say that, if it feels safe. If not, it's OK just to think it.

e. Parents and their grown-up friends should be polite about each other in front of their children.

Finally, the leader has the children discuss briefly what are appropriate amends or restitution in each situation, e.g., apologies, promises not to repeat the offense, repair of the damage, punishment, and promises to try harder in the future.

E2. Review of Jobs and Snack (For younger children)

CLINICAL NOTE: The focus here is on concretely clarifying boundaries and identifying what is right and expectable in family relationships.

While the younger children are eating snack, the role plays are reviewed on the monitor. The leader's questions should include the following:

a. What is the child trying to do here?

b. Is this a kid's job?

c. Is this a parent's job?

The leader checks against the chart and notices whether the child is doing his or her job. If the child is doing more than is expected, the leader notes this and affirms the moral or good intentions. The leader helps the children to decide whether doing extra is getting in the way of their doing their customary jobs. The leader notes that the child/parent may be trying to do the right thing, but is going about it the wrong way and breaking the rules on how we should treat one another. The leader may ask, "Is it OK to scream, push, insult, ignore others' views, hurt others' feelings, etc.?" From this discussion, new rules are generated which are written on the chart. Finally, the leader briefly discusses what are appropriate amends or restitution in each situation, e.g., apologies, promises not to repeat the offense, and repair of damage.

CLINICAL NOTE: When discussing role plays of real-life situations, it is important not to further tarnish the child's view of a parent. It is important to note that:

Everyone is allowed to make mistakes. No one is perfect.

Sometimes when people are angry, upset, or under a lot of stress, they do and say things that they shouldn't.

It is also important to save the child's "face" when it was determined that he or she had broken the rule/principle, by giving lots of credit and appreciation for honesty, good intentions, or lack of knowledge.

F. Closure and Housekeeping

The leader collects name tags and any artwork that the children produced. The leader makes sure that the work has the child's name on it, and places it in the appropriate folder. The leader identifies the camera person for the next session.

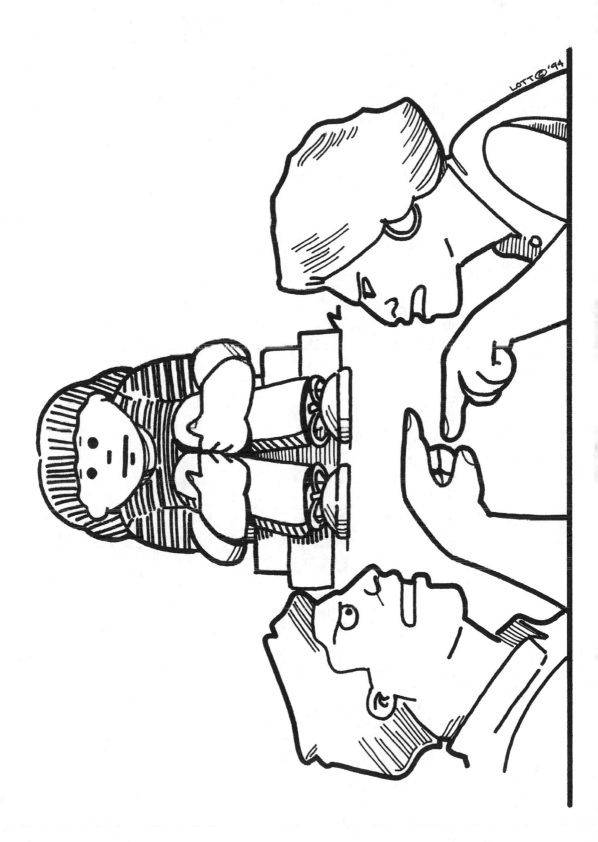

SESSION VI

EXPLORING THE MIRROR
Who You Are and How You Show Your Feelings

GOALS

1. To encourage self-definition and understanding in a safe inner space

2. To help the children understand the difference between feelings and action

MATERIALS

1. Video camera and monitor.

2. Rules chart (posted in group room).

3. Feelings/Color Chart developed in Session I (posted in group room).

4. Name tags and folders (to be kept in leader's possession).

5. Plenty of paper, pencils, markers, and rulers.

6. Feelings Measure Charts developed in Session II (from each child's folder).

PROCEDURE

A. Relaxation

The leader says a brief word of welcome to the group in general and acknowledges each child individually while distributing name tags and noting who will be the camera person today. Then the leader says in his or her own words:

OK, let's see where those shoulders are today. Try to hunch up to your earlobes and then relax. Again.

Leader briefly encourages group to note places of tension and to deliberately tighten up arms, legs, etc., then let go. Leader then says in his or her own words:

Now I'm going to count down from 10 to 0. While I do so, I want you to relax, breathe in—[Pause]—and breathe out—[Pause].

Leader counts slowly from 10 to 0, gently encouraging the group to relax and breathe deeply. When group is relaxed, leader proceeds to the Mirror activity.

B. The Mirror. *For groups that are visualizing, instructions begin here. For groups that are drawing only, go directly to B1 below.*

CLINICAL NOTE: This exercise is designed to encourage the children to define and understand themselves more clearly and to think about who they want to be in the future.

Leader says in his or her own words:

Now you are at the door to your private room. [Pause] Now you go in. [Pause] Has the room changed at all from last time? [Pause] Is it the same? [Pause] Take a little time to walk around in your mind and notice the things you had decided to put in this private place. [Pause] Notice how nice it is that no one can come in and bother your things! [Pause] Now, as you look around, you will see a mirror on one wall of your room. It may be new. [Pause] Decide if your mirror is large or small. [Pause] Does it show only your face? [Pause] Or your whole body? [Pause] Is the mirror fancy? [Pause] Or plain? [Pause] Now you can get fairly close to the mirror. Is it light or dark? [Pause] Can you see well or not? [Pause.] Take a look in the mirror now. [Pause] Is it hard to look at yourself? How do you feel as you do this? [Pause] Do you get tensed up? Try to relax. [Pause] Try to pay attention to what you like about yourself in that mirror. [Pause] Is there anything you would like to change? [Pause] What would you like to change now, or as you get older? [Pause] Maybe you would just like to get a good look. Some kids have a hard time seeing themselves clearly. Take time to do that now. [Pause] Now I'd like you to get ready to leave your mirror. Before you do, take a last look. Pay attention to what you saw that you liked. You may be surprised. [Pause] Pay attention to anything you have promised to change. You might be surprised by that, too. [Pause] Now, I'm going to count up from 0 to 10. Try to stay relaxed as I do so, and then we can draw or write a little about our mirrors.

Leader counts gently and slowly from 0 to 10, and then distributes paper and markers. Leader invites the group to draw what they saw or to list what they liked and what they'd like to change. After 10 minutes or so (or when the group begins to lose focus), invite anyone who wishes to do so to share what they have drawn or written. Have children put their names on their work, and collect and place it in the folders.

B1. The Mirror. *For groups that are drawing only, instructions begin here.*

Leader says in his or her own words:

I want you to imagine for a minute that you are looking in a mirror. Or, if you like, just remember the last time you saw yourself in the mirror. Try to think about what you like about yourself in that mirror. Is there anything you'd like to change? Anything you'd like to change now, or as you get older?

Leader then invites the group to draw what they saw or to list what they liked and what they'd like to change. These productions can be attached to the pictures of internal rooms, collected, and placed in each child's folder.

C. How to Act on Feelings

CLINICAL NOTE: Focus is on helping the children to understand that feelings need not always be expressed in action. It is in the domain of action that control is possible.

Leader distributes Feelings Measure Charts from Session II and says in his or her own words:

You may remember that we talked about feelings in our second meeting and I recall . . .

It is important for the leader to recall briefly some information about each child's participation in that activity at that time. *The children's sense of being heard, understood, and kept in mind in this way is very important.* Leader then says:

Feelings are never wrong. People can't help what they feel. It's important to know how you feel, and it's important to know how other people feel.

However, there are right and wrong ways to act on your feelings. For instance, it's wrong to hit or beat up on someone just because you're mad at them. There are wise and unwise ways to express your feelings, such as, telling your teacher she or he is stupid is probably not a good idea. And there are helpful and unhelpful ways to express your feelings. For instance, sometimes running away when you are scared helps and sometimes it doesn't. Telling a lie when you are afraid of getting into trouble does not help and usually gets you into even more trouble.

Leader then invites the group to identify one helpful or unhelpful way that they may have acted on a feeling that they listed on their Feelings Measure Charts from Session II.

D. Role Plays of Feelings and Actions

Leader asks the group to come up with situations (at home or at school) where someone had strong feelings and acted on them in a wrong or unhelpful way. The leader has the children role-play and videotape the situation, then asks them to do a second role play, showing a better way of expressing those feelings in that situation. The group continues with role playing in this manner until about 15 minutes before the end of group.

E. Snack and Discussion

While the children are eating snack, the leader finishes up the role-playing activity with a summation of five facts:

1. Feelings and behavior are different, so feelings are hard to figure out.
2. Sometimes people hide their feelings and act one way when they feel another.
3. Sometimes people freeze up like rocks when they are afraid of their feelings.
4. There are right and wrong ways to act on your feelings.
5. There might be safe ways to show your feelings, either to a safe person or just to yourself in your own private space.

F. Closure and Housekeeping

The leader collects and labels all work from the session and places in children's folders. Collects name tags and designates a camera person for the next session.

SESSION VII

EXPLORING YOUR INSIDE SELF AND YOUR OUTSIDE SELF

GOALS

1. To help the children to define and understand the difference between an inside self and an outside self

    Feelings get masked but are still there

    It is possible to decide why, when, and how to mask feelings

MATERIALS

NOTE TO LEADER: MATERIALS STARRED WITH AN ASTERISK ARE REPRODUCED IN THE MANUAL AT THE END OF THE SESSION.

1. Video camera and monitor.

2. Rules chart (posted in group room).

3. Feelings/Color Chart developed in Session I (posted in group room).

4. Name tags and folders (to be kept in leader's possession).

5. Plenty of paper, pencils, markers, and rulers.

*6. Blank figure: Two pieces of paper stapled back-to-back, each with an identical blank figure; one set for each group member plus extras for mistakes or revisions.

7. Blank white paper dinner plates.

*8. Sheet of Faces with Different Expressions.

PROCEDURE

A. Relaxation

The leader says a brief word of welcome to the group in general and acknowledges each child individually while distributing name tags and noting who will be the camera person today. Leader briefly encourages the group to note places of tension and to deliberately tighten up arms, legs, etc., then let go. Leader then says in his or her own words:

> Now I'm going to count down from 10 to 0. While I do so, I want you to relax, breathe in [Pause] breathe out [Pause].

Leader counts slowly from 10 to 0, gently encouraging the group to relax and breathe deeply. When leader determines that all the children are sufficiently relaxed, she or he proceeds to the The Statue activity.

B The Statue

CLINICAL NOTE: This activity is designed to encourage children to think about whether and how they show their inner self to others.

For groups that are visualizing, the instructions begin here. For groups that are drawing only, go directly to B1 below. Leader then says in his or her own words:

> Now you are at the door to your private room. Notice how well you are getting to know your own special place. [Pause] Has the room changed at all from last time? [Pause] Is it the same? [Pause] Now, as you look around, you will see, in a kind of dark corner, a statue or sculpture of yourself as you really are. [Pause] Slowly, there is more light and you can discover more about the statue. [Pause] Is it small or tall? [Pause] What shape is it in? [Pause] What is the statue doing? Walk all around and look at the statue. Now I want you to imagine that you have become this statue. [Pause] Imagine that you are this statue. [Pause] What do you do? [Pause] Now become yourself again and look at this statue. [Pause] Does the statue seem any different to you now? [Pause] Has anything changed? Slowly, get ready to say good-bye to the statue and come back to the group as I count up to 10. [Pause] Say good-bye to your statue now.

Leader counts up slowly from 0 to 10 and then invites each group member to become their statue again, for the group, and tell briefly what it is like to be a statue and what the statue does when it comes to life.

B1. The Statue. *For groups that are drawing, instructions begin here.*

Leader says in his or her own words:

I want you to imagine for a minute that you are a statue. Try to imagine what kind of statue you would be. What shape? What size? What is the statue doing? Now draw that statue.

Leader then invites each group member to become their statue and tell briefly what it is like to be a statue and what the statue does when it comes to life.

C. Inside Me/Outside Me

CLINICAL NOTE: Focus is on helping the children to define and understand the difference between an inside self and an outside self.

Leader says in his or her own words:

We're going to be talking a bit more today about how we show feelings. Let's just do a little exercise to get started.

Leader holds up sheet showing faces with different expressions and asks the group to try to identify the feeling each face expresses.

CLINICAL NOTE: It is important to emphasize that not everyone may agree about what the feeling is and that it is not always possible to tell, from the outside, what the inside feelings are.

Leader then says in his or her own words:

Today we are going to think a bit about how we all keep some of our feelings inside; how what we show other people and what we really feel inside are sometimes different. Usually we do that to feel safe or because we think our feelings are not OK. Everyone does it. Right now I want you to remember something that happened in your own family that made you feel like hiding your feelings. You don't have to share it right now. I want you to think about you in that memory. Maybe you are remembering a family meeting, or the day your parents told you they were getting divorced, or the day someone came to visit. Whatever. Think about yourself in that memory. Where were you? What were you wearing? What were you doing? Were you inside or outside? Was the day warm or cold? Remember whatever you can. When you have done that, think about how you felt. Look at the feelings on our Feelings/Color Chart. Which ones fit for you? Did you have a lot of feelings? Did you have mixed feelings?

Now I want you to take the two stapled pieces of paper with blank figures on them. Use our Feelings/Color Chart and fill in these feelings from your memory on the figure on the bottom sheet of paper. These are your inside feelings.

When you have done the inside feelings, think about how you acted at the time of your memory. Were you quiet? Were you noisy? Did you cry or look sad? Did you go away and think about something else? Did you get angry or smile? Think about whether or not you let your feelings show. Now take your outside figure, the one on the top sheet, and fill it in, showing us your outside feelings. Sometimes they're the same as inside feelings, sometimes they're not.

CLINICAL NOTE: Younger children may produce the same feelings on the inside and on the outside. Older children who are anxious may do the same. What is valuable is introducing the idea that the inside and the outside may be different.

When the task is complete, children are invited to share their productions.

D. Masks and Role Plays

CLINICAL NOTE: Focus is on helping the children to become aware of what they present to others and what they mask. Also to consider when, where, and with whom it is safe to remove the mask and be real.

Masks. The leader distributes paper, pens, and paper dinner plates to each child. The leader says in his or her own words:

Sometimes we put on a face (like one of those we saw earlier) to hide our real feelings inside. Let's call this "using a mask."

The leader asks the children to give the reasons why we sometimes hide our real feelings or use a mask (e.g., to avoid hurting other people's feelings, to stop someone from being angry at you, to get someone to give you something you want, to please other people, to keep your own real feelings private). Leader may suggest more concrete ideas such as:

Grandmother comes and brings awful cookies.

You just stepped in something stinky, but you don't want your friends to know.

Your puppy just chewed up the rug. You just found it, and now your mom or dad walks in!

It is important for the leader to emphasize that masks are valuable. The leader is not to challenge the mask in any way, rather the leader is to help the children become aware of their masks so that they can be used effectively.

The leader then asks children to think of a situation (at home or at school) where they used a mask. The leader asks the group to think about what their real feelings were underneath and what kind of face or outside feelings they showed to others, then instructs the children to make masks of their outside faces using colored pens and paper dinner plates. After this is completed, the children may show each other the masks they have made and explain a bit about the situation where they remembered using them. The leader asks the children to identify some of their real feelings underneath (using the Feelings/Color Chart as a prompt).

Role Plays. The leader invites volunteers or encourages the children to take turns role-playing the real-life situation using the masks. The instructions are for the child to play himself or herself holding the mask in front of his or her face. Every so often during the role play, the child removes the mask (which is a signal for the other role players to freeze), looks directly at the camera, and says how she or he really feels. Then the mask is replaced and the role play continues. These role plays are videotaped.

E. Snack and Review of Role Plays

During the snack, the video segments of the role plays are reviewed and discussed. The leader encourages the children to talk about why the masks were needed. Reasons may include the following: to keep from hurting another's feelings, to get someone's cooperation, to keep something private. In addition, the leader may ask the group to generate a list of situations where the use of a mask is questionable (e.g., to lie or to get something you want at the expense of another. Also the leader may comment that if you hide your true feelings all the time, people don't really know you, you can be very lonely, and other people can't give you what you really want; that when you please others all the time and never please yourself you might feel as if you don't matter at all, and you forget how to take care of yourself, etc.).

F. Closure and Housekeeping

The leader collects and labels all work from the session and places in children's folders, then collects name tags and designates a camera person for the next session.

Inside Me/Outside Me

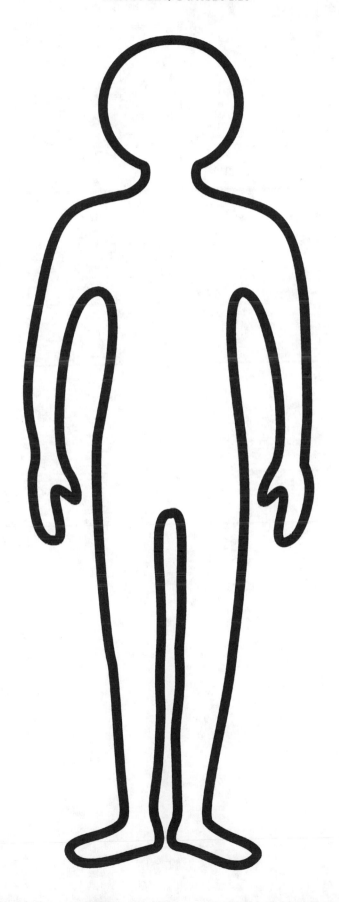

Faces with Different Expressions

SESSION VIII

MAKING A FAMILY SCULPTURE
Who We Are and Who We Could Be

GOALS

1. To help the children to be more conscious of choices about who they are and will become

2. To help the children to consider using their safe inner place in situations outside of group

3. To help the children to begin to anticipate the end of group

4. To help the children to become aware (and more in control) of their positions in their families and their rules and expectations about relationships

MATERIALS

NOTE TO LEADER: Materials starred with an asterisk are reproduced in the manual at the end of the session.

1. Video camera and monitor.

2. Rules chart (posted in group room).

3. Feelings/Color Chart developed in Session I (posted in group room).

4. Name tags and folders (to be kept in leader's possession).

5. Plenty of paper, pencils, markers, and rulers.

6. Small paper cups (two for each group member).

*7. Two apple seed cutout shapes for each child (one to use, one for extra), large enough to have two or three sentences printed on them.

PROCEDURE

A. Relaxation

The leader says a brief word of welcome to the group in general and acknowledges each child individually while distributing name tags and noting the camera person for the day. Then leader says in his or her own words:

> After today, we will have two more meetings together and then we'll go our separate ways for a few months. After that, we'll get to meet together once more, just to check in and say hello and see how we're all doing. Today we're going to spend some time thinking about how you can use your private room when you aren't in group, like when you're at home, at school, or alone. First let's try to relax.

Leader briefly encourages the group to note places of tension and to deliberately tighten up arms, legs, etc., and then let go. After a few moments, when leader feels group is relaxed and focused, they can proceed to Keys to the Room activity.

B1. Keys to the Room. *For groups that are visualizing only*

CLINICAL NOTE: This exercise is designed to help children to understand that they can access a private inner space both in and outside of group. It is also designed to help children begin to think about who they are becoming and how they may influence that process and outcome.

Leader says in his or her own words:

> Now you are going to visit your private room. I'm going to count down from 10 to 0. While I do so, I want you to relax and breathe in [Pause]—breathe out [Pause].

Leader counts slowly from 10 to 0, gently encouraging the group to relax and breathe deeply. Leader then says in his or her own words:

> Now you are at the door to your private room. Notice the size and shape of the door. [Pause] Notice the color of the door. [Pause] Now you are ready to enter this place that has become your own. [Pause] Has the room changed at all from last time? [Pause] I want you to give yourself a chance to think about this room that you have made for yourself at the age you are now. Notice the colors, the mirror—Remember the mirror? [Pause] The gift? [Pause] The

blackboard? [Pause] You may wish to come into this room even when you are not meeting with the group, at times when you are at home or in school or alone and you just need a safe place to be with yourself. [Pause] Look around you—this room will always be here for you, now and even as you get older. It is a safe and protected place. [Pause] Now let's get ready to leave our rooms, but just for a moment, because we'll be coming back a couple of times. We'll practice getting in and out of this room whenever we need to. [Pause] I'll count slowly from 0 to 10. While I do so, you will leave your rooms, gently close the door, and then come back to us in the group.

Leader counts from 0 to 10, intermittently instructing the group to slowly leave, close the door, etc., then says:

Now let's practice getting to our own safe places when we want to. I will start you off, and then you will do a couple of trips to your room alone. Notice how you get yourself into your room space.

B2. A Wish for Tomorrow. *For groups that are visualizing, the instructions begin here. For groups that are drawing only, proceed directly to B3 below.*

Leader counts down slowly from 10 to 0 and guides the children back to their private rooms, then says in his or her own words:

OK, now you're back in your room. I want you to think about who you will be when you are 21 years old. [Pause] What will you be doing? [Pause] How will that person be the same as you are now? [Pause] How will that person be different from who you are now? [Pause] Now I want you to make a promise to that 21-year-old. It can be a promise about anything that has to do with helping you become what you want to be when you are 21. It is a private promise, and it is safe because you are making it in your private room. [Pause] Now I want you to imagine that you are placing that promise to yourself in a seed that you will plant in your room. [Pause] That seed will grow as you grow. [Pause] Now imagine that you are planting your seed with the promise inside it. [Pause] And you are placing it in a safe place in your room. [Pause] Now I will count back up from 0 to 10. While I do so, you will slowly leave your room again and rejoin the group.

When finished counting, leader asks the children to write their promise on the paper seed provided, fold it, and drop it into their paper cup.

B3. A Wish for Tomorrow. *For groups that are drawing only, the instructions begin here.*

Leader says in his or her own words:

> Now I want you to think about who you will be when you are 21 years old. What will you be doing? How will that person be the same as you are now? How will that person be different? Now I want you to make a promise to that 21-year-old. It can be a promise about anything that has to do with helping you become who you want to be at age 21. It is a private promise. Now I want you to write that promise on this paper apple seed and then plant it in your Dixie cup. As you plant, imagine that this promise will grow with you. You may wish to draw the growing seed on the picture of your room.

C1. Family Sculpture (older children)

CLINICAL NOTE: The goal of the exercise is to help the children to make conscious their role in their family as well as their rules and expectations about relationships. This perspective can help the children to revise their rules and expectations in a more realistic way.

Leader asks the group to explain what a sculpture is (e.g., a piece of art that shows feelings and ideas in a form that you can see and touch). Leader explains that "In this session we are going to use our bodies to create a sculpture to explain our feelings and ideas."

Warm-Up. Split the children into small groups of three or four (it might be useful to divide the boys from the girls) to practice making sculptures using their body positions and facial expressions to represent the following contradictory feelings and ideas:

a. Feeling in charge, like you can do what you want, vs. feeling helpless, like you have to do what another person wants

b. Feeling close vs. feeling far apart

c. Hoping, praying that the other person will do what you want vs. giving up and ignoring the other person, or pretending you don't care

d. Feeling like you belong and keeping someone close to you vs. feeling like you don't belong and feeling left out

e. Feeling embarrassed vs. feeling proud

f. Fighting and arguing vs. agreeing and cooperating

g. Doing something wrong and feeling bad vs. punishing someone else and feeling mad

The small groups take turns in representing, in still-life form, each of these scenes and guessing what is being represented. Next the leader has the group members sit around the table with paper and pens, and asks them to map out a sculpture of their family.

Children can elect to do part or the whole of their family situation, and some might choose to do two sculptures (one with their dad and one with their mom). The children may or may not play their own part in the family sculpture. The leader encourages expression of feelings about closeness/distance, inclusion/exclusion, conflict/cooperation, etc., in these scenarios. The children then take turns in setting up each family sculpture, which is then videotaped from all angles (1–2 minutes for each).

C2. Family Sculpture (younger children)

The leader says in his or her own words:

Today we're going to do some work being statues. We're going to make groups of statues that show opposite feelings. Let's talk about opposites for a minute. What is the opposite of "Up"? "Tall"? "Happy"? OK. Now we're going to try to show how opposite feelings, like happy and sad, might look if they were statues.

The small groups take turns representing, as group statues, each of these scenes, holding them for 30 seconds or more. Next the leader has the group members sit around the table with paper and pens and draw how they usually are with their family.

Leader asks in his or her own words:

What would each member look like if they were part of this group statue?

CLINICAL NOTE: If children are struggling with this exercise, leader may modify the instructions for some or all group members, to draw how they usually are with one of their parents. Other children might choose to do two sculptures—one with Dad and one with Mom.

The children may or may not play their own part in the family sculpture. The leader encourages them to express their feelings about being close or far apart, being left out or belonging, fighting or getting along, etc. The children then take turns in setting up each group statue, which is then videotaped from all angles (take 1–2 minutes for each).

D. Fantasy Family Sculpture

When the videotaping of each sculpture or group statue is completed, the leader starts with the first sculpture and asks the child who set it up:

> How would you change this to make it just the way you wish your family could be?

Leader can prompt that this may involve ejecting certain members, bringing others in, or rearranging them in some way. The changed grouping is then videotaped from all angles.

> ADDITIONAL CLINICAL NOTES: The ultimate goal is to help the children to identify their particular rules and expectations about relationships, e.g., "In your family you have decided: don't have feelings; don't make demands; always be in control; be the central pivot that stops the family from falling apart; don't get too close to anyone; I am no good; etc." Be warmly supportive and careful with any interpretation, emphasizing that this is an understandable way to feel and act: "You are just trying to survive; trying not to hurt your dad's feelings; trying not to get your mom angry at you; trying to take care of your mom; trying to be different from your brother; etc."

Caution: These family sculptures can arouse powerful feelings in the children which, if not properly supported and worked through, can lead to anxiety and distress, acting out, or phobic avoidance when the child goes home or in future sessions. It is often helpful to predict that upsetting feelings may occur and invite the children to talk about them in a separate individual session.

E. Letter to Parents

> CLINICAL NOTE: This activity is designed to affirm child's sense of self and boundaries.

Leader takes poster board or paper and pen and labels it "Things I Want You to Know About Me." Leader says in his or her own words:

> Now that we've thought about what it's like to be in our family, let's write a

letter to all the moms and dads who are fighting and might be getting a divorce. We won't mail it; it is private, it is ours. We will list all the things we want them to know about us and our families.

Leader facilitates and serves as scribe. When the letter is complete, all the children should come up and sign it.

F. Snack and Review

During snack time, the children review their family sculptures on the video monitor. As each family scene is reviewed, the leader asks each child to talk about what feelings and ideas the sculpture represents, how each of the members is feeling, with special focus on the child. Questions to help the child process this experience might include the following points:

a. "What would you like to do in this situation?"

b. "If you weren't in this family, how would it be different?"

c. "If you spend a lot of time with your friends, will anything be different at home? Will your family be there for you when you get back?"

d. For children who have produced two entirely different, uncoordinated scenes, in Mom's and Dad's houses, ask them to imagine one parent's household as audience to the other scene, and vice versa : "Is this OK, to allow both Mom and Dad to watch what you are doing at the other parent's house?"

G. Closure and Housekeeping

The leader collects name tags and any artwork the children have produced. The leader makes sure that the work has the child's name on it and places the work in the appropriate folder. The leader identifies the camera person for the next session and reminds the group that there will be two more sessions after today.

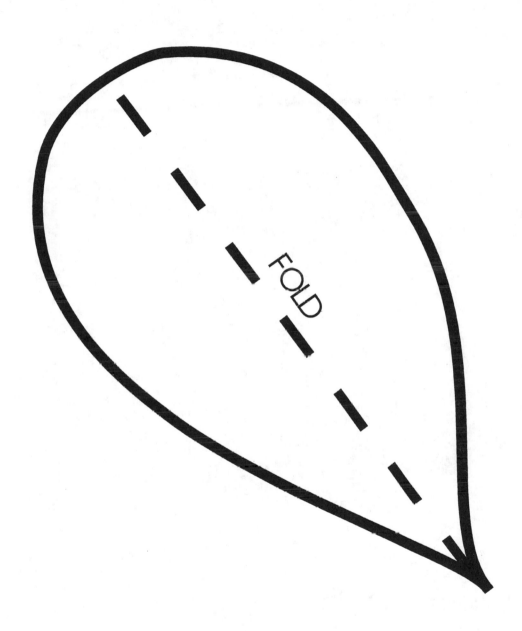

FOLD

SESSION IX

BECOMING THE EXPERTS ON LIVING WITH CONFLICT

GOALS

1. To encourage children to see their peers as potential resources and sources of support

2. To encourage children to share different ways of coping with dilemmas that are common in conflicted families

3. To help the children to make moral decisions about how to resolve these dilemmas

MATERIALS

NOTE TO LEADER: Materials starred with an asterisk are reproduced in the manual at the end of the session.

1. Video camera and monitor.

2. Rules chart (posted in group room).

3. Feelings/Color Chart developed in Session I (posted in group room).

4. Name tags and folders (to be kept in leader's possession).

5. Plenty of paper, pencils, markers, and rulers.

6. Two or three balloons, straws, Scotch® tape, glue, fabric scraps, Dixie cups, dry macaroni, and other materials appropriate for a small group sculpture.

*7. Panel of Experts Questions/Sample Letters from Other Kids. (These are developed by the leader for older groups and should reflect specific issues that members have shown, during group sessions, that they are struggling with.)

*8.   **Dilemma-Situations Pictures.**

9.   **Family roles/rules and principles charts generated during Session V.**

PROCEDURE

A. Group Art Project

CLINICAL NOTE: The focus of the activity is to have children experience mastery through cooperation with their peers.

The leader goes around the table, makes a brief statement of welcome to the group in general, and acknowledges each child individually while distributing name tags and noting the camera person for the day. The leader then says in his or her own words:

Today we're going to spend some time helping each other. You might find that other kids can be a big help sometimes, when you're stuck or when you just want to have some fun. Other kids, who are outside your family, can be really important in your life and can sometimes help you get over bad times when the family feels shaky. We'll start with a helping project.

The leader distributes materials for the group art project equally (see Item 6 in Materials section). Leader explains that the group will have 10 minutes in which to build a statue of a person, plus any other figure or things, in such a way that all the materials that have been distributed are included in the statue and are added to the statue by the person who has possession of them. The rules are that the group may not speak, although they may communicate nonverbally (leader may need to demonstrate), and the group members may trade materials with other group members at any point if both agree. Leader begins timing when the project has been clearly explained. When the project is finished, the leader should comment positively on the statue and on the group members' ability to help each other make something so creative, unusual, etc. Leader should ask the group's permission to keep the statue to show other children their age who might not know, as well as this group does, how to work well with other children and get things done.

B1. TV Panel of Experts (for older children)

CLINICAL NOTE: The focus of the activity is to consolidate new ideas about relationships and to encourage children to see their peers as a resource.

Leader says the following in his or her own words:

> Because you all have parents who sometimes/often have problems with cooperating, you have become something of an expert on how kids feel about parents' fighting. You also have a lot of good ideas on how kids can cope with the problems that come up. We are going to make a TV show, where you will be the panel of experts like on————[give examples of TV shows]. You are going to answer questions asked by other kids whose parents fight or are getting divorced.

To heighten the seriousness of this task, the leader can also explain that not only parents but also other adults, like judges, attorneys, mediators, counselors, and teachers, often really don't understand how children think and feel when parents fight or split up and that their answers will be an important way of teaching these adults. The leader explains that if the children give their written permission, he or she would like to use some of their words (but not their names) when talking to these adults as well as to other children.

Warm-up. The leader reads the first one or two questions or letters (from examples in the list at the end of the session) and has the children practice their responses. The group then decides on a name for the TV program, e.g., "The Wide World of Divorce" or "The Wide World of Families," and assigns a camera person and a talk-show host.

The show begins with an introduction of the panel by the host, and the children give their first names and the number of years their parents have been separated/divorced/or in conflict. Then the talk-show host asks two or three questions (per segment), generating lots of discussion and alternative coping strategies among the group.

Each segment of the show is punctuated by short commercial breaks that the children make up. After each commercial, the talk-show host and camera person are rotated.

B2. Solving Dilemmas (for younger children)

The prompts for discussion and role plays consist of the series of pictures that are included in the manual at the end of this session. The leader should select one of these pictures at a time (or substitute a new one, according to what would be appropriate and useful for the children in any particular group).

Discussion. The leader says in his or her own words:

Take a look at this picture. [Show picture] What is happening here? What do you think the child is feeling? What do you think each adult is feeling? Did anything like this ever happen to you?

Leader then asks in his or her own words:

What do you think the child should do here?

Leader generates lots of alternative coping responses, talks about different outcomes for the different coping responses (i.e., evaluating the alternatives), and helps the group to decide on one of the better solutions.

Role Play. Have the children role-play the dilemma and the solution. Videotape this production. Ask if they feel OK about the solution and if not, why not?

Repeat this process with as many of the different dilemmas portrayed as time permits. (The leader can alternate between simply discussing the picture and deciding on solutions, and actually role-playing, depending on the interest of the group.)

C. Snack and Review

CLINICAL NOTES: Focus of the activity is to clarify and affirm the rules of moral conduct in relationships.

During snack, the video segments of the Panel of Experts are reviewed. This task naturally raises many moral dilemmas, which the children are prompted to address in further discussion. For older groups, the leader notes how the children's responses accord with the rules of moral conduct that they have generated in previous sessions.

For younger groups, it is important to validate different kinds of coping responses in different situations, e.g., assertive efforts, strategic withdrawal and avoidance, or seeking the help of others. It is also important for children to differentiate between what they can and cannot solve.

D. Closure and Housekeeping

The leader collects name tags and any artwork the children have produced, makes sure that the work has the child's name on it, and places the work in the appropriate folder. The leader identifies the camera person for the next session and reminds the group that there will be one more session after today.

Examples of Panel-of-Experts Questions*

1. My parents cannot agree about how much time I spend with each

of them. Sometimes I feel like I have to decide, but that's really hard. What could I do?

2. Sometimes I feel like my mom loves me too much, like she won't let me out of her sight or something. I love my mom, but I love my dad and having my own life too. What should I do?

3. I wish my mother would spend more time with me than she does. How can I let her know how much she is hurting my feelings?

4. My parents fight all the time. I feel like I have to take sides because, if I don't, they might not want me around. What do you think I should do?

5. My parents act like they're totally in charge of the visitation schedule, and I don't get to say what I want. Like, sometimes I want to just hang out or just get some attention on my own, for myself. What should I do?

6. My stepdad thinks he's supposed to be in charge of me, but he's not. I don't like him. What can I do?

7. After my parents got a divorce and I saw how my dad treated my mom, I decided all men are creeps. What if I can never find a man to marry who is not a creep? What can you tell me about that?

8. My mother blames my dad for everything that goes wrong, and I wish that she would stop. What can I do about this?

9. My parents play favorites with us kids. When I'm the favorite, I feel sort of happy, but sad and mad that my brother is not the favorite and that he's mad at me about it. What can I do about this?

10. Sometimes I think that neither of my parents really wants me around. Got any ideas about that?

*These examples were generated by a group of children who were concerned with divorce. Other groups may have very different concerns (e.g., levels of violence, safety, drug and alcohol use).

Picture A for Session IX

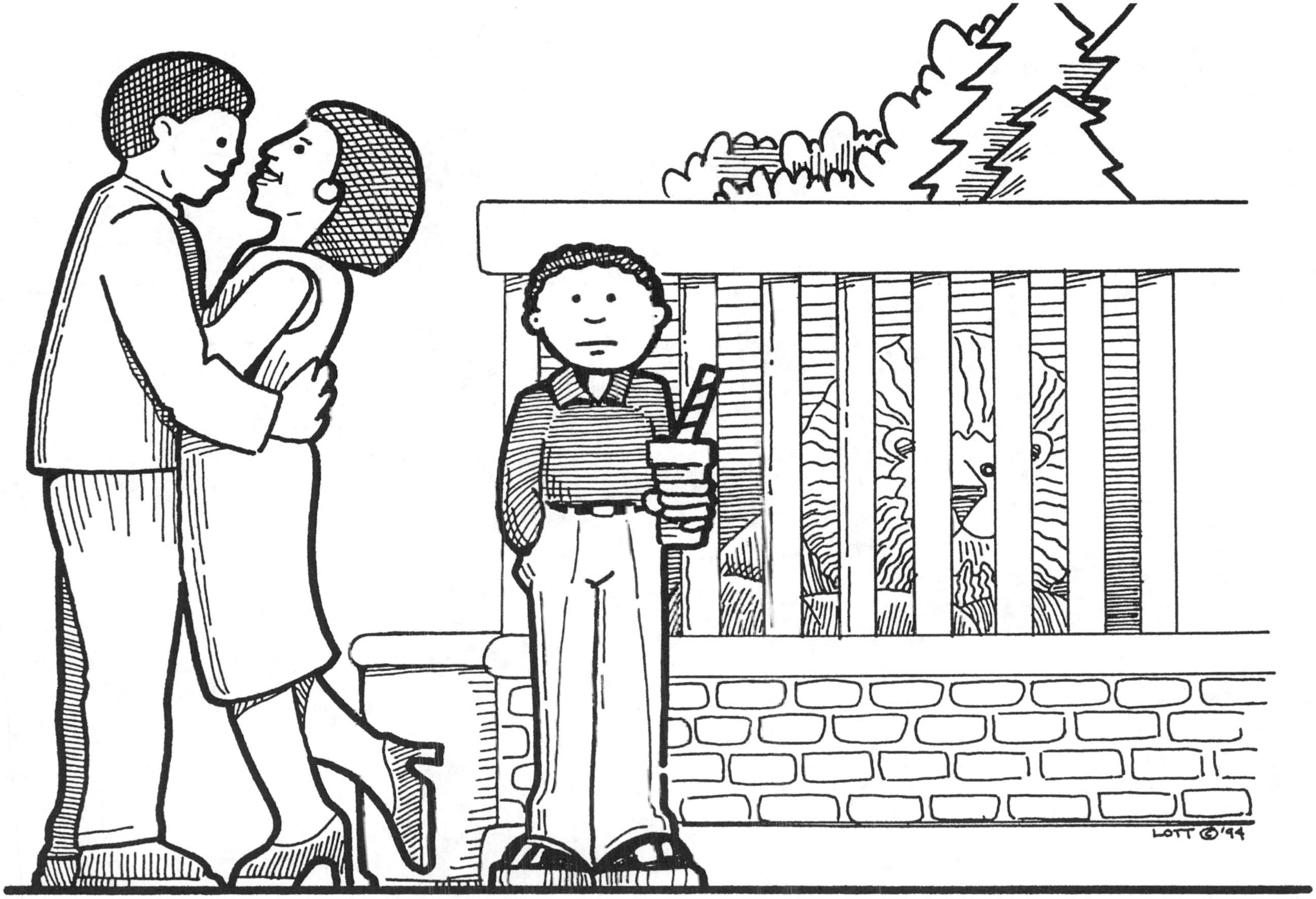

SESSION X

TELLING YOUR STORY SO FAR, THINKING ABOUT WHO YOU WANT TO BE IN THE NEXT CHAPTER, AND SAYING GOOD-BYE

GOALS

1. To suggest that there can be a coherent story in many family conflicts

2. To help the older children to identify with or distance themselves from different aspects of both their parents in a conscious way

3. To help the younger children to consider how to love and remain attached to both their parents

4. To achieve a sense of closure in the group and to say good-bye

MATERIALS

NOTE TO LEADER: Materials starred with an asterisk are reproduced in the manual at the end of the session.

1. Video camera and monitor.

2. Rules chart (posted in group room).

3. Feelings/Color Chart developed in Session I (posted in group room).

4. Name tags and folders (to be kept in leader's possession).

5. Plenty of paper, pencils, markers, and rulers.

*6. "The Turtle Story."

*7. Identity Shields (for older latency groups only). You will need

> sheets of white cardboard (11" x 8") for each child, with an outline for a coat of arms drawn on each sheet; colored pens, pencils, scissors, and glue.

*8. **An Award Certificate for each child.**

9. **Party food.**

PROCEDURE

A. Story of the Divorce ("The Turtle Story")

CLINICAL NOTE: The purpose of this exercise is to reduce confusion and anxiety by providing children with a way to organize their understanding of parental conflict without blaming or taking sides. The leader may decide to reword the story to reflect concerns of children in a family that is in conflict but does not divorce. See alternative ending 2 for example.

Children are asked to make themselves comfortable (lean back and close eyes). If possible, they can lie on a rug on the floor. Leader says in his or her own words:

> Now we are going to visit our private rooms once again. Try to relax your shoulders, your whole body. [Leader encourages the children to relax further by deliberately tensing and relaxing their muscles.] Now count yourself down from 10 to 0. [Pause for about 30 seconds] [Add the following only for groups who are visualizing: Notice now that you are at your door and can enter your special room whenever you're ready. (Pause) Notice how your room is always there for you. (Pause) Is it warm or cold? (Pause) Get comfortable in your room.] Now I will tell you a story.

Leader narrates (or reads) "The Turtle Story" (see the end of the session). The leader asks the children whether they know why their parents got married/got together in the first place (what attracted them to one another), what changed over time, and what made them start to fight or separate.

CLINICAL NOTE: Some children will be able to explain this better than others. Some may not be very interested. Don't push it with those who can't or don't want to explain this. Invite those who are confused but interested to talk about it further with parents, or with the group leader in individual sessions, if possible.

B1. Identity Shields (for older children)

CLINICAL NOTE: The purpose of this exercise is to introduce the idea that identifications can be consciously selected. The idea is to create a shield that shows what each child is striving for, an *ideal that sets a standard* rather than an expectation of unrealistic perfection.

The leader distributes the coat of arms on cardboard to each child. Leader says in his or her own words:

Each of you is beginning your own life's journey—going on a big adventure. You'll soon be teenagers and growing up. You want to be prepared for this special journey, a mission into the future, by taking things with you from your past. This includes different things from each of your parents (like being a land turtle and a sea turtle), from other special people you have known— or would like to know—as well as pieces that are uniquely you. You may also want to deliberately leave behind things that are not useful—from each of your parents and from these other people. There may also be parts of yourself you might like to leave behind.

What you have in front of you is a shield for a coat of arms that will represent what you want to take with you in your journey into life. Notice that your coat of arms is divided into five parts. The top left-hand corner represents your mom, the top right-hand corner represents your dad, the two middle sections are for any two people who have been important to you in your life, and the bottom piece is you.

Using words or pictures, write or draw what you want to take with you from each person. On the blank area outside the shield, write or draw what you want to leave behind.

The children can keep their coats of arms private if they wish, or they might like to share them with the other group members at the end. When they have finished drawing, they are instructed to take the scissors and cut out the coat of arms, leaving the remainder behind. Note: It is important to collect all the pieces later (including the discarded parts) so that the group leader can reconstruct and assess what each child did.

B2. "Turtle Story" Role Play (for younger children)

CLINICAL NOTE: This activity is designed to help younger children apply the ideas that are introduced in "The Turtle Story" to their understanding of their own family.

The leader invites the children to reenact "The Turtle Story" from beginning to end, acting out all the feelings that each of the turtle family members had, especially Tommy and Tina.

If time permits, this role play can be repeated with different children playing the role of the young turtles. Children are invited to elaborate on the story in any ways they wish. Their productions are videotaped. If there is time at the end of this activity (30 minutes should be set aside for the closing sections of this session), the children can watch the videotapes and talk about the different feelings the young turtles had and how they expressed these feelings in the different role plays.

C. Wrap-Up and Review of Folders

Leader distributes folders and says:

Today is the last meeting that we will have together.

When appropriate, the leader should invite the group to review the contents of the folders.
(CLINICAL NOTE: Themes and ideas that may have recurred.)

Leader should then share some of his or her feelings about the end of the group, e.g., having enjoyed the group, missing the group members in the future, believing in their future, and, possibly, noting that it is hard to say good-bye.

D. Awards

Leader distributes an Award Certificate to each child and notes that each award is different and personal. Each Award Certificate should be in an envelope or made private in some other way, and each child's award should reflect some positive quality in that child. The leader should attempt to reinforce authentic qualities, such as effort, bravery, or honesty. (Award Certificates are available in stationery stores, or the example shown at the end of this session may be reproduced.)

E. Snack and Closure

During snack time, it is a good idea to create a list of names and phone numbers for each child. The leader should make available the same number of blank sheets as there are children. Each child starts a list with his or her own name and number and then passes it to their neighbor. End the session at a clearly specified time.

F. Follow-Up

If the parents of the children in the group were not participating in their own parent group, then the leader distributes a letter to each parent at this time, listing whatever continuing services might be available to the children. The list should be as specific as possible; for example, if additional groups are going to be run, the leader should specify the dates and times (even if these are approximate). Names and phone numbers of individual counselors or agencies in the area should be included, with some reference to the fee schedule if possible. After the letter is distributed, the leader should follow up with a phone call or meeting with the parents in which the leader provides individual recommendations for follow-up for each child.

The Turtle Story

Once upon a time, there was a sand turtle named Sammy. Sammy lived in the sand by the ocean, just near the edge of the woods. Every day he loved to lie in the sun on the sandy beach. He also liked to make tunnels and secret hideaways in the sand dunes. His favorite food was sand crabs. Nearby in the ocean there was a sea turtle whose name was Sally. Sally lived deep down in the ocean and loved to frolic and swim in the waves. She loved to feel the cool blue-green water on her body as she hunted for jellyfish to eat.

One day Sammy the sand turtle crawled to the water's edge to look for sand crabs. At the same time, Sally the sea turtle swam to the shallow part of the beach where she could poke her head out of the water to see the blue sky. All at once Sally and Sammy's eyes met and they fell in love. Sally had never seen a sand turtle before, and she thought he looked different and handsome in his dark brown shell. Sammy had never seen a sea turtle before, and he thought Sally's blue-green shell was so different and just the prettiest he had ever seen.

The two turtles loved each other so much that they decided to get married. For a time they lived at the water's edge so that Sammy could sit on the sand and keep warm and dry while Sally sat in the shallow water to keep cool. Pretty soon they had two baby turtles, named Tommy and Tina. These little baby turtles had very nice brown and blue-green shells. They looked something like each of their parents.

Tommy and Tina Turtle loved to play in the sand with their father, Sammy. They would spend hours digging tunnels and searching for sand crabs to eat. Sometimes they would take naps side by side in the warm sand. When they pulled in their heads and legs, their shells looked like rocks sticking halfway out of the sand. Tommy and Tina also loved to frolic in the sea with their mother, Sally. They did somersaults in the waves and explored the underwater caves and reefs, looking for jellyfish for dinner. For a while this was a happy family of turtles.

But then something went wrong! Tommy and Tina Turtle were having so much fun that they didn't notice that Sammy, the father sand turtle, was spending less and less time at the water's edge. He wandered up into the sand dunes and hunted for food near the edge of the woods. Sally, the mother sea turtle, spent all her time swimming in the deep part of the ocean, and she did not sit in the shallow water on the beach anymore. Each night, when the father and mother turtles met to feed the kid turtles some dinner, they would argue and fight. Sometimes Sammy the sand turtle and Sally the sea turtle snapped at each other. Tommy and Tina were scared they might hurt each other. Sometimes the mother and father turtles refused to talk to each other. Sammy, the father sand turtle, would pull his head into his shell and dig into the sand, and Sally, the mother sea turtle, turned her back on him and dove into the ocean.

Alternative Ending 1 (focus is on separation and divorce).
[If parents have not separated, the story should continue here.] Finally one day, Sammy and Sally decided they didn't want to live together anymore. Sally decided to live at the bottom of the ocean, and Sammy decided to live up in the sand dunes above the beach.

Tommy and Tina Turtle were very sad. They were still young turtles and needed someone to look after them. They loved both their mom and their dad and wanted to be with both of them all the time. Tommy was kind of angry, and he yelled a lot and had fights with his mom. Tina was angry, too, but she kept her feelings inside and hid in her shell all day. She wouldn't even play with her brother or any of her friends. Most of all, Tommy and Tina Turtle wanted their parents to live together at the water's edge and to be a happy family again.

One day they decided to ask the Wise Old Owl to help them. The Wise Old Owl always gave good advice to all the animals, and he could fix almost any problem. Early the next morning they packed a picnic lunch and set off for the forest to look for the Wise Old Owl. He was sleeping in a tree when they arrived, but he woke up and invited them into his tree stump for a visit. Very soon they told him the problem. Tina Turtle then asked, "Can you make our mother and father live together again?" And Tommy Turtle said, "Please, please make them love each other again!"

The Wise Old Owl stared thoughtfully into the sky for some time and then he said: "It's very difficult for a sand turtle and a sea turtle to live together. They are two different kinds of turtles, and they need different kinds of homes. Sammy the sand turtle likes to dig in the sand and sit in the warm sun. But Sally the sea turtle likes to dive down deep under the ocean waves and swim in the cool blue water. When they tried to live together at the water's edge, they were both unhappy, cross, and angry. It was too wet and cold for Sammy and too dry and hot for Sally. It is much better that they each live in the place where they can be happy and have the things around them that they need.

"But you, Tommy Turtle, and you, Tina Turtle, are each half sand turtle and half sea turtle. You can live in the cool ocean and eat jellyfish *and* you can live on the warm sand and eat sand crabs. You can have fun with your mother and you can also have fun with your father. They love you very much and they want you to be happy. The best plan is for you to live some of the time in the water with your mother and some of the time on land with your father."

And that is just what Tommy Turtle and Tina Turtle did! Sometimes they lived in the deep blue ocean and practiced their swimming with their mother, and sometimes they lived on the warm, sunny sand and practiced hunting in the dunes near the woods with their father. They made lots of friends with all the fish and dolphins and whales in the ocean, and they made lots of friends with the deer and the badgers and the foxes that lived in the woods. They loved their mother and they loved their father. In fact, Tommy and Tina Turtle became happy again and grew up to be very special turtles, with beautiful brownish-bluish-green-colored shells that were remarkably fine looking and exceptionally sturdy. The Wise Old Owl said this was probably because they had made the best of living in two different worlds, and everyone agreed that this was so.

Alternative Ending 2 (focus is on ongoing conflict or violence).
CLINICAL NOTE: The leader may make further modifications or additions (including creating a synthesis of both alternative endings) to meet the needs and experiences of the group participants.

Sammy, the father sand turtle, would pull his head into his shell and dig into the sand, and Sally, the mother sea turtle, turned her back on him and dove into the ocean waves. This went on for a long time, and it was hard for Tommy and Tina to bear. Tommy got kind of angry and yelled a lot and had fights with other kids and with Tina. Tina was angry, too, but she kept her feelings inside and hid in her shell a lot of the time. Most of all, Tommy and Tina wanted the fighting to stop.

One day the young turtles decided to ask the Wise Old Owl to help them. The Wise Old Owl always gave good advice to all the animals, and he could fix almost any problem. Early the next morning they packed a picnic lunch and set off for the forest to look for the Wise Old Owl. He was sleeping in a tree when they arrived, but he woke up and invited them into his tree for a visit. Very soon they told him the problem, and Tommy Turtle said, "Please, please make them stop fighting and love each other again!"

The Wise Old Owl stared thoughtfully into the sky for some time and then he said: "It's very difficult for a sand turtle and a sea turtle to live together. They are two very different kinds of turtles, who need very different things. They might learn how to stop fighting, but they will certainly need help from someone who is wise. They can come to me or to another owl in my family if they want, but they have to make the journey themselves. Neither you, Tina, nor you, Tommy, can do it for them, no matter how much you may want to help.

"If there is a lot of fighting, you might want to go to your neighbors the seagulls, or your friends the badgers, or the blue dolphins, for help from animals who are big and strong. You might need to go inside your shells to stay safe some of the time, but you don't have to stay there all the time. Remember, there are other things that young turtles like to do and can do. You, Tommy Turtle, and you, Tina Turtle, are each half sand turtle and half sea turtle. You can live in the cool ocean and eat jellyfish *and* you can live on the warm sand and eat sand crabs. You can live your own lives in peace. You can love your mother and your father and still want to have a different kind of life when you grow up. You can make a solemn promise to yourselves that when you become grown-up turtles, with beautiful brownish-bluish-green-colored shells, you will make a family of your very own where no one needs to feel afraid."

Tommy and Tina felt that this was good advice. They were very, very quiet for a long time. They could hear the birds singing in the forest and feel the sun shining down. Then, without saying anything, Tina walked quietly up to the Wise Owl and said, "Owl, will you hear my promise, and keep it for me until I am big?" The Owl nodded; he understood that this was very, very important. Then Tina bowed her head and took a deep breath and said, "I, Tina Turtle, do solemnly promise that I will grow up and make a peaceful family, where no one needs to be afraid. I will always remember how sad and mad the fighting makes me feel now. The memory of these feelings and the Owl will help me to remember my promise always." Tina sighed a big sigh. She felt better and stronger than she had ever been. Then it was Tommy's turn. He too went up to the Wise Owl and said, "I, Tommy Turtle, do solemnly promise that I will grow up and make a peaceful family, where no one needs to be afraid. I will always remember how sad and mad the fighting makes me feel now. The memory of these feelings and the Owl will help me to remember my promise always." Tommy sighed and smiled at Tina. He too felt stronger now. Then they thanked the Wise Owl and began the rest of their lives.

Sometimes they played in the deep blue ocean and practiced their swimming with their mother, and sometimes they spent time on the warm, sunny sand and practiced hunting in the dunes near the woods with their father. Sometimes they all did things together. Those were good times. Sally and Sammy learned how to work things out some of the time. Sometimes they still had fights. Those were not such good times. When this happened, Tommy and Tina stayed together and mostly kept their heads in their shells, which was very smart of them. Sometimes they would go swimming in the ocean or running in the forest to get out some of the mad feelings. Every once in a while they got help from seagulls or dolphins, which was also very smart of them. When they got older they went out swimming or hunting with their friends, and that made life feel very good. Tommy and Tina grew up to be very special turtles who remembered their promise to the Wise Owl all their lives long. They were remarkably fine looking, exceptionally sturdy, and, most of all, they were peaceful and unafraid.

Identity Shield for Duplication

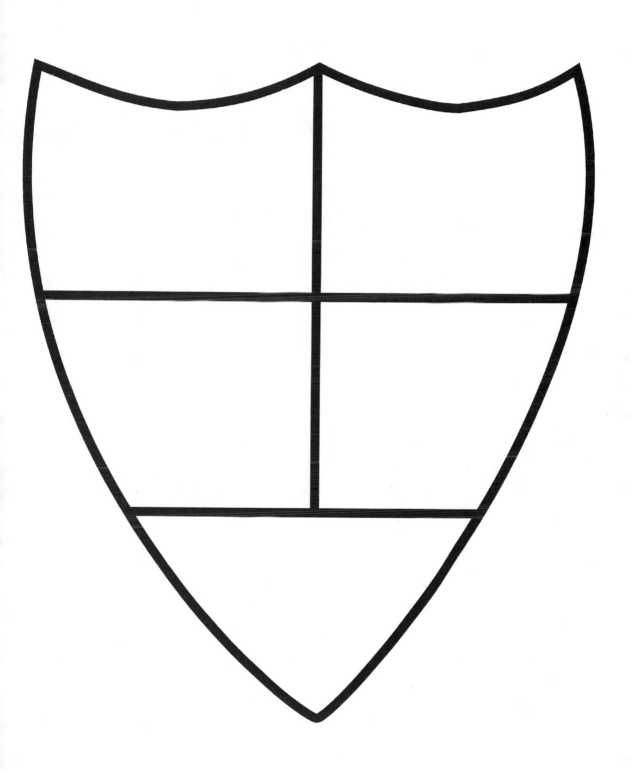

Certificate of Distinction

in Recognition of

For Distinguished Achievement in

APPENDIX A

TROUBLESHOOTING SECTION

I. STRATEGIES FOR PREVENTING MANAGEMENT DIFFICULTIES

Use intake and screening to:

1. Identify children with well-documented histories of acting out in groups. The leader will need to decide if there are enough resources (coleaders, extra time for planning or holding conferences) to manage this child in the group. If not, the child is not a good candidate.

2. Identify, to the degree possible, an optimal balance of boys to girls and a mix of life experiences and personalities.

3. Identify the issues that the children are concerned with. This will help the leader to identify the right mix of children who have similar histories as well as pictures, activities, and questions that will keep the children involved.

4. Decide whether the group will need one or more leaders. When in doubt, and another leader is available, it is best to use two leaders because it is hard to predict how the children will react.

Pick the right group room.

Sometimes there will be no choice about the room, but it is important to work thoughtfully with what is available:

1. Try to make the room a protected place. People who are not in group should not be able to come in or hover around the group room during group.

2. Limit distractions. Cover windows, unplug phones, remove toys that are not used in group, keep snack out of room until snack time.

3. Try to use a table and chairs for structured activities as well as a rug area for unstructured activities.

Prepare carefully before every session.

All leader instructions to the group are designed to be said in your own words, so it is important to be very familiar with what is to be communicated. Also, it may be necessary to substitute activities or stimulus pictures for role plays which are more relevant to the needs of the particular group. All of this takes planning. Groups quickly lose focus when the leader is unprepared or must pause to find materials.

Provide materials to keep hands busy during discussion or sharing:
1. Crayons, pictures from coloring books, or plain paper can be available for children to color with.
2. Modeling beeswax can be available for shaping.
3. Yarn can be available for finger knitting.

II. STRATEGIES FOR MANAGEMENT WHEN THE GROUP IS UNFOCUSED OR OUT OF CONTROL

Use a seating plan.

Use a fixed seating plan at the group table to help separate children who distract each other. The plan should be flexible—change it as necessary. When the group is losing focus, have them return to their seats. At that point it may be useful to begin a silent activity.

Change the atmosphere.

Leader can dim some of the lights or lower his or her voice until the group refocuses.

Move ahead to videotaping.

Set up a rule that the camera goes on only when there is calm, otherwise the group is wasting time and film. When that expectation is in place, the group will often calm down because they want to go on camera.

Change the content to keep it relevant to the children's culture and concerns.

If stimulus pictures for role plays don't capture the concerns or cultural realities of the children in the group, use different ones that do. Photographs may be found in news magazines. (Be careful not to use material that is more violent or frightening than anything the children may have referred to. Photos that *suggest* the children's concerns are preferable [e.g., police officers entering or leaving a house is preferable to police using weapons or restraints]. Pictures may be found in books for children. Examples include:

1. People who are sick
2. People (adults or peers) with guns or knives
3. People (adults or peers) physically hitting
4. Police entering a home
5. Police taking a family member out of a home
6. Families being evicted
7. Families being separated

Slow down when children are having a hard time understanding what to do.

When children are immature or highly traumatized, they may be very concrete. Many of the ideas in the sessions will be new. Keep the instructions very simple, and use a lot of demonstration. Use activities for the younger groups, even with older groups.

Get active when the children seem bored.

The leader can pick up the pace by limiting sharing and discussion and going to the active part of the work more quickly.

Change the intensity level to limit anxiety.

The group may become restless and distractible because the material is raising too much anxiety. Leader may need to shift to a more controlled way of working:

1. Work silently. Many of the activities can be done without any words, as charades. This provides greater control and containment.
2. Work with puppets. Many of the activities can be done with puppets. This provides more distance and can prevent the children from becoming flooded with too much feeling.

Use a token economy.

Screening information may help the leader to determine ahead of time whether this kind of management is necessary, or it can be introduced after the group begins. Rules include:

1. At the beginning of group, each child receives a regular snack coupon and two tokens.

2. Regular snack coupons can never be taken away. All children receive regular snack unconditionally.

3. Bonus tokens are used to purchase additional snack items at the end of each session.

4. Each additional snack item is worth two bonus tokens.

5. Leader awards bonus tokens to children who are working hard and following the rules, to a maximum of four tokens per session.

   If children repeatedly violate group rules, it may be necessary to add a consequence to the token economy.

6. For specific violations of group rules, the leader may give one warning and then take a bonus token away. The child may earn it back, or purchase half a snack item if he or she is left with one bonus token. Remember, the regular snack coupon is never taken away.

III. Strategies for Helping Individual Children to Stay Focused and in Control in Group

Avoid time-out.

Time out is *not an appropriate* strategy for these children, who are likely to become panicked about being abandoned. If a child needs to be removed, it should only be with a coleader who can stay with the child and help him or her to calm down and return to the group.

Stay close.

Allow a coleader to stay close to a child who is having trouble; a gentle hand on the back or shoulder can sometimes bring calm and help the child to know that an adult is there to contain him or her.

Provide special responsibilities.

Some children have a particular capacity to lead their peers into distractions. Such a child's leadership abilities can sometimes be redirected. He or she may be given the role of assistant leader. Responsibilities may include distributing and collecting materials, taking charge of a timer for timing, or selling snacks if a token economy is being used.

Meet with the child's parents.

Set up a conference with the child's parents to decide if it is possible for him or her to continue in group. If it is decided that the child will continue, develop a behavioral contract. Use positive-reinforcement techniques in the contract whenever possible.

If a child must be expelled from group.

Removing a child from group is always a last resort, but it is sometimes necessary. When this happens, it is important for the leader to explain the reasons why the child could no longer be in group in terms that are neutral, respectful, and compassionate. The other children will need time to talk about their feelings as soon as possible. They may wish to write the child a group letter of support in order to create closure.

IV. STRATEGIES FOR PRESERVING GROUP SAFETY

If a child is accidentally hurt.

The leader has a serious responsibility to ensure that group is safe and controlled. Still it is not always possible to avoid accidental injuries when children are involved in boisterous activity. If this happens, it is important for the leader to keep in mind how anxious these children are likely to become about this momentary loss of safety. They will need to see that the leader handles the situation calmly and that the injury is carefully nursed. If another child is responsible for the injury, the leader can use the episode as an opportunity to help him or her to acknowledge responsibility and make appropriate amends (e.g., helping to fix the injury, making an apology) without losing face.

When a child becomes too aggressive in the role play.

A child may get so involved in an aggressive role that he or she may seem frighteningly out of control to the other children. When this happens, the leader *must intervene immediately* to preserve the sense of safety in group. The leader can have the child freeze in role, and allow the other role players to identify their feelings and the feelings that they read in the aggressive child's body posture and face. For example, the leader may say, "OK, Tommy, let's freeze that for the camera and find out how it looks to your audience." This needs to be done with care. This is not an attack but an opportunity for an aggressive child to notice his or her impact on others. The aggressive child can then be empowered by new directions. The leader can say, for example, "Let's take the action down a notch, and see how it looks" or "Let's say, in the role play, that you noticed the others were scared, how would that change the action? Let's see that."

When a child offers a fantasy of violent revenge in a follow-up role play.

This represents an opportunity for the leader to notice the strong feelings that are the basis of the fantasy. The feelings must be acknowledged. The leader can then discuss, in matter-of-fact terms, what would happen if the fantasy were actually acted out, what rules of moral conduct would be violated, how this would be for the child, and so on. The leader can identify the negative consequences to the child in a supportive way, and also help the group to look at the difference between feeling solutions and real world solutions that lead to enhanced coping.

V. STRATEGIES FOR ADDRESSING ISSUES IN INDIVIDUAL TREATMENT

Distrustful, avoidant children.

Help the child to make the avoidance concrete, so he or she can work with it in therapy. To do so, encourage hide-and-seek games in the therapy room or in the sand tray, using masks, sunglasses, screens, tunnels, barricades, and other hiding places. Allow the child to build a secret place that can be entered only at his or her invitation. A variation of Blind Walk (Session II, B) may be appropriate. Also Inside Me/Outside Me (Session VII, C) and Masks (VII, D) can be useful.

Anxious, controlling children.

Allow the child as much control as possible in order to reduce his or her anxiety and need for distance. Allow him or her to sit in the therapist's chair. Ask permission for any intervention that is made. Negotiate the agenda for the session, allowing plenty of room for activities that provide respite from the work. Use guided imagery and other relaxation techniques (see Session IV, A–VIII, A).

Concrete, dispirited children who cannot use fantasy.

In general, it is useful to treat these very constricted children as if they were younger than their actual age. Begin with concrete work that orients the child in time and place. Identify the details of a visitation schedule, and make a calendar, discussing who lives where, including pets. Make a time line with the child that shows a chronology of important events in his or her life, people that have come and gone, age at divorce or remarriage. Draw a family tree, and describe who is related to whom. Use the Fantasy Room (Session IIIA) and related activities (Session IV, B–VIII, B) to help the child toward more self-awareness. Use List of Feelings (Session I, D) and Color Feelings (Session I, E), and Level of Feelings (Session II, C) and Charade of Feelings (Session II, D), to help to make feelings seem less overwhelming. Jobs for People in Your Family (Session V, C) may also be appropriate.

Children who engage in repetitive play sequences.

This can happen when children cannot find release from rigid ideas, rules, and expectations about the way relationships work. The therapist may choose to interpret the child's feeling of being stuck or intervene directly by suggesting different directions or endings to the play. If the child rejects the intervention, the therapist can ask why these endings are not possible. The never-ending quality of the play may reflect the never-ending quality of the family conflict. If this is so, the child's reality must be acknowledged within the play or directly.

Children who become frightened and disrupt their own play and fantasy.

The therapist will need to help the child to modulate and slow down the play. Provide soothing, nonarousing alternatives (e.g., card or board games, throwing a ball through hoops) to help calm the child after a disruption. (Note carefully what content the child disrupts, because it is likely to be diagnostic of central fears and conflicts.)

Children who become overwhelmed, regressed, or out of control.

Use smaller play equipment requiring finer motor coordination. Use figures (e.g., animals, not people) to create more distance. Encourage the child to take control of the out-of-control actors and animals in their play. Help the child to identify the rules and become the director, the king, Superman. Help the child to bring in army or police figures to quell a riot. Remind the child of the rules of the playroom when it is necessary or as a way to provide reassurance. Technically, it is better to predict and avoid the child's escalation to the point of being overwhelmed if at all possible.

APPENDIX B

PSYCHOEDUCATIONAL GROUPS FOR PARENTS

The lasting value of the children's experiences in groups depends in large part on the effectiveness of collateral work with their parents. Here the goals are to heighten the parents' capacity to perceive and respond to their children's needs separately from their own and enhance their motivation to make decisions and agreements that protect the children from further conflict. These goals can be addressed quite effectively when the children's group leader also convenes psychoeducational groups for parents at intervals during the program. In this format, the leader can provide the parents with information about the effects of family conflict in general and then translate these general issues into more specific concerns of individual children. In a sense, the meetings resemble group parent-teacher conferences in which the teacher (leader) describes the curriculum as it pertains to the needs of the class (group) and then focuses on the strengths and weaknesses of the individual student. In the psychoeducational group, as in the parent-teacher conference, it is the leader's direct experience of the child that makes him or her credible to the parent. In this dual role, it is important that the leader protect the children's confidentiality. In general, this means that the leader is free to discuss his or her impressions of the child's needs, concerns, and coping style but does not directly quote the child or share writings or drawings that are produced in group without the child's permission.

Psychoeducational group meetings may be convened at the beginning, in the middle, and toward the end of the children's program (which involves weekly sessions over a ten-week period). In order to maximize parents' attendance, the meetings can be scheduled to follow the children's sessions, and child care is provided. Scheduling also permits highly conflicted parents to participate separately. A child's father, for example, might attend parent group meetings scheduled for the first, fifth, and ninth weeks of the program, while the child's mother might attend during the second, sixth, and tenth weeks.

The work begins with education. Here the leader establishes the commonality of the parents' experience with chronic conflict and provides information about its effects on children in general. A working metaphor can provide an effective framework for understanding. For example, the child's sense of self can be likened to a tapestry that cannot be woven into a whole design without the horizontal (mother) and vertical (father) strands to hold it in place. Even when one or both strands are of poor quality, they cannot be ripped away without unraveling the whole design. Instead it is the design itself that must be strengthened.

Once this kind of working frame of reference is in place, the leader describes subtle signs of distress in school-age children and explains why some youngsters seem to show no signs at all. This explanation focuses on how children learn to "keep from unraveling inside" or to function "as double agents in a militarized zone," becoming guarded and overcontrolled in their efforts to maintain appearances and predict what will be required of them. Here the leader particularly emphasizes the ways in which children's efforts to achieve safety and control can leave them feeling as if they are not completely real and unable to form authentic relationships with anyone. With this information on the table, the leader can begin to help parents to understand how these coping efforts can undermine children's self-esteem and limit their ability to mature in their understanding of themselves, other people, and relationships. This provides a foundation for explaining how a working agreement between parents can support the children by providing a predictable environment that protects their children's involvement in life beyond the conflict and outside the family.

Once the leader has communicated these general points, the individual children become the focus of discussion. The leader frames his or her comments as observations that the parent is invited to confirm or interpret differently. In a discussion of the children's need to maintain appearances, for example, the leader may say, "I've noticed that both Jane (your daughter) and John (your son) try really hard to get things perfectly right. It seems as if it's hard for them to take risks. For instance, one of them had trouble making a drawing without a ruler and lots of erasing. I wonder if it's hard for them to make mistakes. Do you [either parent] notice this in your child? What do you make of it?" This approach can help the parent to focus on the child, without undermining his or her parental authority or competence. Parents' responses to these kinds of questions often lead to discussions of the causes of the child's difficulties. Some parents begin to see themselves and their role in the conflict more clearly when they recognize themselves in the points of view of others. Others benefit from feedback that group members provide with a kind of directness and authority that comes from shared experience. When this happens, it is the leader's responsibility to maintain a safe and constructive tone in the group discussion. Throughout the parent meetings, the leader also helps the parents to anticipate and support the kinds of changes that take place in the children as they work in group. This is particularly important because a number of children do become more curious, assertive, and even rebellious as they find their own voice. These shifts can be difficult for parents to understand, tolerate, and manage appropriately without information and direction from the group leader.

For some parents their experiences in the psychoeducational group are enough to leverage their disengagement from the conflict and their commitment to developing and honoring coparenting agreements. This kind of outcome depends on the capacity of the parents to assimilate information about their child as an individual and to gain insight into their own role in the conflict. More vulnerable parents generally benefit in a more circumscribed way, achieving (though not always maintaining) a limited degree of insight and a conceptual framework for understanding conflict and its effects. It is this framework that can become the foundation for additional work in therapeutic group mediation (see Johnston and Campbell, *Impasses of Divorce: The Dynamics and Resolution of Family Conflict*, Free Press, New York, 1988, for a more extensive description of this approach) or in individual sessions.

ADDITIONAL READINGS

Hodges, W. F. (1986). *Interventions for children of divorce: Custody, access and psychotherapy.* New York: Wiley.

Johnston, J. R., & Campbell, L. (1988). *Impasses of divorce: The dynamics and resolution of family conflict.* New York: Free Press.

Johnston, J. R., & Roseby, V. (1997). *In the name of the child: A developmental approach to understanding and helping children of conflicted and violent divorce.* New York: Free Press.

Kurdek, L. (1986). Children's reasoning about parental divorce. In R. D. Ashmore & D. M. Brodzinsky (Eds.), *Thinking about the family: Views of parents and children* (pp. 233–276). Hillsdale, NJ: Erlbaum.

Roseby, V., & Deutsch, R. (1985, Spring). Children of separation and divorce: Effects of a social role-taking group intervention on fourth and fifth graders. *Journal of Clinical Child Psychology, 14,* 55–60.

Roseby, V., & Johnston, J. R. (1995). Clinical interventions with children of high conflict and violence. *American Journal of Orthopsychiatry, 65,* 48–59.

Roseby, V., & Wallerstein, J. (1997). Impact of divorce on latency age children: Assessment and intervention strategies. In P. Kernberg & J. Bemporad (Eds.), *Handbook of child and adolescent psychiatry*, vol. 2, pp. 181–201. New York: Wiley.

Selman, R. (1977). A structural-developmental model of social cognition: Implications for intervention research. *Counseling Psychologist, 6* (4), 3–6.

Selman, R. (1980). *The growth of interpersonal understanding.* New York: Academic Press.

Wallerstein, J., & Kelly, J. (1980). *Surviving the breakup: How children and parents cope with divorce.* New York: Basic Books.

INDEX

About the Authors

Vivienne Roseby, Ph.D., is Director of Protecting Children from Conflict at the Judith Wallerstein Center for the Family in Transition. She is on the consulting faculty at the University of California at Davis Child and Family Studies Center and in private practice. She lives in Davis, California.

Janet R. Johnston, Ph.D., is Executive Director of the Judith Wallerstein Center for the Family in Transition and Associate Professor at San Jose State University. Dr. Johnston is coauthor of *Impasses of Divorce: The Dynamics and Resolution of Family Conflict* (Free Press, New York, 1988) and coauthor of *Through the Eyes of Children: Healing Stories for Children of Divorce* (Free Press, New York, 1997). She lives in Menlo Park, California.

Vivienne Roseby and Janet R. Johnston are coauthors of a companion volume, *In the Name of the Child: A Developmental Approach to Understanding and Helping Children of Conflicted and Violent Divorce* (Free Press, New York, 1997).

ALSO OF INTEREST FROM THE FREE PRESS

In the Name of the Child: A Developmental Approach to Understanding and Helping Children of Conflicted and Violent Divorce
Janet R. Johnston and Vivienne Roseby

"A major advance in the understanding and treatment of children caught in the torment of parental conflict. With clarity and compassion the authors report the impact of witnessing fighting and violence on emotional, intellectual and moral development, together with new healing methods that they have developed over many years. Essential reading for judges, family attorneys and all mental health personnel who work with divorce. This book changes the field."

> —Judith S. Wallerstein, Ph.D, author of *Second Chances: Men, Women, and Children a Decade After Divorce*

1997 ISBN: 0-684-82771-9

Through the Eyes of Children: Healing Stories for Children of Divorce
Janet R. Johnston, Karen Breunig, Carla Garrity, and Mitchell Baris

Written by leading authorities on child psychology and divorce, this book is a valuable and much needed tool for parents and professionals who work with children struggling with family breakup. Relying on imagination and metaphor, the original stories and illustrations in this unique anthology provide a safe and effective way to help children understand and cope with their parents' separation and living apart. For generations, stories have been a foundation for teaching children. *Through the Eyes of Children* continues that tradition and allows children the chance to recover and heal from divorce.

1997 ISBN: 0-684-83703-X

Impasses of Divorce: The Dynamics and Resolution of Family Conflict
Janet R. Johnston and Linda E. G. Campbell

"Battles over children take place on many fronts, but custody is the critical campaign. . . . Johnston and Campbell have thrown themselves into the midst of such divorce feuds as mediators, clinicians, and investigators. In doing so they have produced a book that is timely, insightful, and practical. . . . The uninitiated will be horrified by the insightful portrayal of the destructive maneuvering carried out in the name of the 'child's best interests.'"

> —*Contemporary Psychologist*

1988 ISBN: 0-02-916621-7